A
SOCIAL PSYCHOLOGY
RESEARCH EXPERIENCE

Second Revised Edition

Jennifer J. Harman, Ph.D.
Colorado State University

Justin J. Lehmiller, Ph.D.
Harvard University

cognella™
San Diego, CA

Bassim Hamadeh, CEO and Publisher

Michael Simpson, Vice President of Acquisitions

Jamie Giganti, Managing Editor

Jess Busch, Graphic Design Supervisor

Becky Smith, Acquisitions Editor

Monika Dziamka, Project Editor

Natalie Lakosil, Licensing Manager

First published in the United States of America in 2014 by Cognella, Inc.

Trademark Notice: Product or corporate names may be trademarks or registered trademarks, and are used only for identification and explanation without intent to infringe.

Cover image copyright © 2008 by iStockphoto.com/ mstay

Printed in the United States of America

ISBN: 978-1-62661-026-2 (pbk)/ 978-1-62661-027-9 (br)

www.cognella.com 800.200.3908

Contents

Purpose and Course Schedule   1

General Course Information   5

Lab #1   10

ETHICAL ISSUES IN SOCIAL PSYCHOLOGY RESEARCH   11

Some Thoughts on Ethics of Research:
After Reading Milgram's "Behavioral Study of Obedience"   13
By Diana Baumrind

Issues in the Study of Obedience:
A Reply to Baumrind   19
By Stanley Milgram

Lab #2   26
Research Ethics in Social Psychology   27
In-Class Ethical Issues Exercise   29

UNDERSTANDING AND SUMMARIZING RESEARCH ARTICLES AND APA FORMATTING   35

How to Read a Journal Article in Social Psychology   37
By Christian H. Jordan and Mark P. Zanna

Lab #3   46
APA Formatting and Style Guide   47
Research Article Summary Homework   51

LITERATURE REVIEWS   53

Lab #4   54
Using PsycINFO   55
Literature Review   57
Homework Assignment: PsycINFO Search   59

NON-EXPERIMENTAL RESEARCH DESIGNS 61

Lab #5 63
Non-Experimental Research Designs 65

EXPERIMENTAL AND QUASI-EXPERIMENTAL DESIGN 67

Lab #6 69
Experimental and Quasi-Experimental Research 71
Lab Group Exercise: Group 1–4 75–78

HYPOTHESIS DEVELOPMENT 79

Lab #7 81
Research Questions 83
Hypothesis Development and Operationalization 85
Hypothesis Development Homework 87

MEASUREMENT 89

Lab #8 91
Measurement 93

SURVEY PROCEDURES 95

Lab #9 97
Survey Procedures 99
More Eyes on the Prize:
Variability in White Americans' Perceptions of Progress Toward Racial Equality 103
    By Amanda B. Brodish, Paige C. Brazy, and Patricia G. Devine

What Does It Mean to Be an American?
Patriotism, Nationalism, and American Identity After 9/11 105
    By Qiong Li and Marilynn B. Brewer

Survey Validation Worksheet 107
Measuring Gambling Outcomes Among College Students 109
    By Clayton Neighbors, Ty W. Lostutter, Mary E. Larimer, and Ruby Y. Takushi

Lab #10 113
Administering Computerized Surveys 115
Operationalization of Hypothesis:
Survey Method 117
Survey Summary Homework 119
Locating a Survey Using PsycINFO 121

PRIMING AND AUTOMATICITY PROCEDURES 123

IAT Exercise 125
Lab #11 127

Priming and Automaticity Procedures 129

Narcissism Beyond Gestalt and Awareness:
The Name Letter Effect 131
    By Jozef M. Nuttin

Automatic Attitudes and Alcohol:
Does Implicit Liking Predict Drinking? 133
    By B. Keith Payne, Olesya Govorun, and Nathan L. Arbuckle

Operationalization of Hypothesis:
Priming or Automaticity Method 135
Study Rationale Worksheet 137
Feedback on Drafts of Paper 139

PSYCHOPHYSIOLOGICAL AND BEHAVIORAL (OBSERVATIONAL) PROCEDURES

PSYCHOPHYSIOLOGICAL AND
BEHAVIORAL (OBSERVATIONAL) PROCEDURES 141

Lab #12 143
Social Psychophysiological Research 145
Physiological Data 149
The Psychophysiology of James Bond:
Phasic Emotional Responses to Violent Video Game Events 151
    By Niklas Ravaja, Marko Turpeinen, Timo Saari,
    Sampsa Puttonen, and Liisa Keltikangas-Järvinen

Social Support in Couples: An Examination of
Gender Differences Using Self-Report and Observational Methods 155
    By Lesley L. Verhofstadt, Ann Buysse, and William Ickes
Behavioral Observation Methods 159
Operationalization of Hypothesis:
Physiological or Observational Methods 161
Behavioral Observation Exercise 163
Behavioral Coding Sheets 165
Behavioral Observation Exercise Summary Sheet 173

SMALL GROUP RESEARCH PROCEDURES

SMALL GROUP RESEARCH PROCEDURES 175

Lab #13 177
Small Group Research Procedures 179
Autocracy Bias in Informal Groups Under Need for Closure 181
    By Antonio Pierro, Lucia Mannetti, Eraldo De Grada,
    Stefano Livi, and Arie W. Kruglanski

Nominal Group Technique, Social Loafing, and Group
Creative Project Quality 185
    By Cheryl L. Asmus and Keith James

Operationalization of Hypothesis:
Small Group Methods 187
Draft of Introduction Section 189

EVENT SAMPLING PROCEDURES 191

Lab #14 193

Event Sampling Procedures 195

The Value-Congruence Model of Memory for Emotional Experiences:
An Explanation for Cultural Differences in Emotional Self-Reports 197
By Shigehiro Oishi, Ulrich Schimmack, Ed Diener,
Chu Kim-Prieto, Christie Napa Scollon, and Dong-Won Choi

When Accommodation Matters:
Situational Dependency within Daily Interactions with Romantic Partners 199
By Nickola C. Overall and Chris G. Sibley

Operationalization of Hypothesis:
Event Sampling Methods 201

Homework Assignment: Summary of Additional Article for the Introduction 203

QUALITATIVE PROCEDURES 205

Lab #15 207

Qualitative Methods 209

Dimensions of Majority and Minority Groups 211
By Viviane Seyranian, Hazel Atuel, and William D. Crano

The Motivational Basis of Concessions and Compromise:
Archival and Laboratory Studies 215
By Carrie A. Langner and David G. Winter

In-Class Qualitative Analysis 219

Operationalization of Hypothesis:
Content Analysis Method 221

Rationale for Method Selected for the Study 223

Revision to Introduction and Draft of Method Section 225

INSTITUTIONAL REVIEW BOARDS 227

Lab #16 229

Institutional Review Boards:
Why We Have Them and How They Work 231

Measurement Worksheet 233

Lab #17 235

IRB Materials 237

Information Typically Required in an IRB Protocol 239

Cover Letter 243

Debriefing Information 245

Lab #18 246

EXPERIMENTAL PROTOCOLS 247

Lab #19 249

Developing an Experimental Protocol 251

Example of an Experimental Protocol:
Myspace Study   253

DATA ANALYSIS AND STATISTICS   255

Lab #20   257
Data Analysis and Statistics   259
Statistics Summary Page   263
Statistical Programs   265

DATA COLLECTION   267

Lab #21   269
Lab #22   270
Lab #23   271
Lab #24   272
Constructing Data Sets for Analysis   273

DATA INTERPRETATION, WRITING, AND DISSEMINATION   275

Data Interpretation   277
Lab #25   278
Running Your Analyses   279
Lab #26   281
Putting Your Statistical Output into Words   283
Draft of Results Section   289
Lab #27   291
Draft of Discussion Section and Abstract   293
Lab #28   295
Research Dissemination   297
Poster Presentations:
An Alternative to the Research Talk   299
Sample Conference Poster   301
Research Experience Journal   303

ORAL PRESENTATIONS   305

Final Presentation Guidelines   307
Lab #29   308
Lab #30   309
In-Class Presentation Grading Criteria   311

Purpose and Course Schedule

THIS course is intended to introduce you to general issues of research in social psychology. This is a hands-on, "nuts and bolts" laboratory, where you will learn **how** social psychologists conduct research: the research questions they pose, and the research methods and procedures they employ. The overall purpose of this laboratory is to give you experience designing, executing, and reporting an experimental study on a social psychology topic. An attempt will be made to meet these ambitious goals through weekly lectures, a series of research exercises, and a research project.

The concepts covered in this class are challenging and the assignments interesting—but demanding. **Expect to dedicate time** to it, and don't fall behind. Students who are successful come to every class, do the assignments, and are active in the learning process.

The format of this class is twofold. We will discuss research methods used to investigate social psychological concepts and theories, and you will work with your fellow students to: (a) review prior research critically; (b) formulate research hypotheses and study proposals; (c) conduct actual research; and (d) report the results of your study.

Course Objectives

1. To learn about a wide variety of research methods and procedures used in social psychological research.
2. To acquire hands-on experience designing and conducting research in social psychology.
3. To think critically about experimental research in social psychology.
4. To work collaboratively with other students on a research project of mutual interest.
5. To develop skills in presenting research proposals and results in social psychology.
6. To extend skills in writing up proposals for future research and experimental results using APA format.
7. To develop skills in programming computers for data collection purposes.
8. To extend skills in using commonly used software packages for statistical analyses.

Recommended Additional Texts (either would be useful, but you probably do not need both)

Publication Manual of the American Psychological Association (6th ed.). (2009). Washington, DC: American Psychological Association.

Schwartz, B. M., Landrum, R. E., & Gurung, R. A. R. (2011). *An Easy Guide to APA Style*. Thousand Oaks, CA: Sage.

Week #	Lab #	Homework Due	Lab Topic	Lab activities
1	1	None	Introduction	Description of course requirements, icebreaker activity.
1	2	Read Baumrind and Milgram; Review Key Terms	Ethics	Discuss articles.
2	3	Read Jordan & Zanna; Bring APA manual	APA formatting and writing	Assign to research topics.
2	4	Research article summary	Using PsycINFO	Discuss research article, develop search terms, identify other background articles.
3	5	Bring in draft summaries of two background articles	Research Design I	Discuss background articles in group.
3	6	Submit final summaries of two background articles	Research Design II	Complete study design activity.
4	7	None	Developing a hypothesis	Quiz (labs 2–6), learn about hypothesis development and operationalization.
4	8	Two hypotheses	Measurement	Learn general measurement issues, discuss possible hypotheses, rank order favorite hypotheses.
5	9	None	Survey methods	In-class questionnaire exercise. Receive final hypothesis from instructor.
5	10	Read Neighbors et al. article. Survey validation worksheet	Locating and administering surveys	Operationalize hypothesis using survey method, locate possible surveys for use in study, learn computerized survey methods.
6	11	Summary of survey; IAT worksheet	Priming & automaticity measures	Quiz (labs 7–10), learn about Inquisit software and other methods of measuring automatic responding, operationalize hypothesis using priming or automaticity measures.
6	12	Rationale worksheet; Outline of paper	Psychophysiological and behavioral observational methods	Physiological experiment demonstrations, operationalize hypothesis using psychophysiological and observational methods.
7	13	Behavioral observation exercise	Small group research	Quiz (labs 11 & 12), operationalize hypothesis using a small group research method.
7	14	Draft of Introduction	Event sampling methods	Operationalize hypothesis using an event sampling methodology.
8	15	Summary of another article for Introduction	Content analysis	In-class qualitative analysis, operationalize hypothesis using content analysis, select operationalization for study.
8	16	Operationalization Rationale; Revision of Introduction and draft of Methods section;	Institutional review boards and obtaining approval for research	Quiz (labs 13–15).
9	17	Measurement worksheet; Online ethics training certificate	Writing an IRB proposal	Work on IRB forms for mock approval.

9	18	None	Finish and submit IRB proposal in class	Finish working on proposal and submit materials to instructor in class.
10	19	None	Revise IRB proposals	Make revisions to IRB proposals, and develop a protocol.
10	20	Experimental protocol; Bring Statistics guide from Library Reserve	Descriptive and differential statistics	Practice using statistical packages.
11	21	Final IRB proposal revision	Mock run-through of experiment	Quiz (labs 16–20). Practice running study with classmates, make modifications, start preparing for data collection.
11	22	None	Collect Data	Class time used to collect data.
12	23	Revision of Introduction and Methods sections	Collect Data	Class time used to collect data.
12	24	None	Collect and/or Analyze Data	Set up data file.
13	25	Have data entered into statistical program	Analyze data	Analyze results.
13	26	Bring statistical output	Interpreting data and writing results	Complete output writing exercise. Learn how to write results. Learn how to present research findings graphically.
14	27	Draft of Results section	Writing the Discussion section and abstract	Learn how to write the Discussion section and abstract for the paper.
14	28	Draft of Discussion section and abstract	Research dissemination & oral presentations	Learn about conferences and how to give oral and poster presentations.
15	29	Research Experience Journal.	Finalizing oral presentation	Continue working on oral presentation with your group.
15	30	Oral presentation ** Final papers due during finals week	Oral presentations	Present research findings to class. Evaluate performance of peers and self.

General Course Information

A note on group work: Your group will be counting on you to do your share of the work. Each person is expected to put in an equal amount of work for each aspect of the research project. The research team ratings exist in order to help ensure that no one is unfairly taken advantage of. In addition to equal contributions, students are expected to stay in regular contact with their group. *If you need to miss classes for any reason, you will still need to be in touch with your group via outside meetings or e-mail.* If you are out of contact with your group for several days (with the exception of official university breaks) without a legitimate, documented excuse (i.e., serious medical illness or emergency), the instructor reserves the right to drop you from your group. If you are dropped from your group, you will receive no credit for any of the group's assignments, including the research paper and oral presentation. Because these assignments make up such a large portion of final grades, students who are dropped from their groups will not be able to pass the class. Thus, it is vital that you stay in touch with your group and do the work that is expected of you.

A note on plagiarism: Plagiarism is a form of academic dishonesty, and any student found plagiarizing will receive academic penalty and possible university disciplinary action. Plagiarism involves copying another person or organization's words, thoughts, or ideas and passing them off as one's own, without giving credit to the original source. Paraphrasing and/or quoting material without properly documenting the source is also a form of plagiarizing. According to Diana Hacker (in *A Writer's Reference*, 3rd Edition), there are three acts of plagiarism: "(1) failing to cite quotations and borrowed ideas, (2) failing to enclose borrowed language in quotation marks and (3) failing to put summaries and paraphrases in your own words."

If your instructor suspects you of plagiarism, you will first be notified, and then will make an appointment to discuss the allegation. After this discussion, it is up to the instructor to decide whether plagiarism has occurred, and if so, an academic penalty will be assigned. This penalty may be a reduced grade on the paper, or a failing grade in the course. The decision can be appealed through the University's Conflict Resolution program, but if the student is deemed guilty, additional disciplinary action may be taken.

Bottom line: Do NOT plagiarize.

Research Project

One of the objectives of the course is to develop and test a research project. Below are five early steps in research:

1. Choose a topic;
2. Review the literature;
3. Determine the research question;
4. Develop a hypothesis;
5. Operationalization.

Over the first several weeks of this lab, you will proceed through these steps. You will work on the last step as we progress through the course. The first task it to select a topic. To aid in this process, you will be given six research topics to choose from. Each topic is described below. The key is to pick one or two that MOST interest you. **You will need to rank order your most preferred project to your least preferred.** This rank ordering will determine the lab group to which you are assigned (approximately four students will be assigned to each lab group).

For ALL possible projects, we have background material for you to read and sample manipulations and measures. There is an advantage in using preestablished materials that researchers have developed. You are welcome to design your own manipulations and measures, however. Once you get in your lab group, you will identify specifically what hypotheses you want to test, and how you want to test them. Your tasks are to:

1. Develop and submit your hypotheses, manipulations, and materials to your instructor for review.
2. Write an IRB proposal and develop materials for IRB review and approval.
3. Prepare for data collection.
4. Collect data.
5. Meet with your instructor to analyze data and get guidance for writing and presenting results.
6. Deliver presentation of results to class (group project).

Topics:

1. **Expression of prejudice**: *Are people more likely to express prejudice when their past behavior has established that they are nonprejudiced persons?*

Monin and Miller (2001) conducted three experiments—and found that yes, people are more likely to express prejudice when they have shown that they are nonprejudiced. A more recent study showed that white adults who know that they are going to write about a controversial racial issue such as Affirmative Action choose first to write about their glowing friendships with people of color.

2. **Terror management**: *Does thinking about one's own death increase the need to believe that others share your worldview?*

Terror management theory (TMT) predicts that people use cultural worldviews, such as religion, personal values and standards, etc., to reduce anxiety about thoughts of death. Many TMT studies have shown that when feeling uneasy, people do a number of mental tricks to regain control over their world perspective. This set of field studies (Pyszczynski *et al.*, 1996) examined whether people walking close to or in front of a funeral home were more likely to believe that others supported their worldviews. They hypothesized and showed that when reminded of death, even when that reminder is outside of direct awareness, people overestimate how much others agree with their own worldview.

3. **Attachment style and relationship social comparisons**: *Are anxious or avoidant people more likely to make relationship comparisons?*

In a study conducted by LeBeau and Buckingham (2008), individuals with anxious attachment styles were more likely to make relationship social comparisons, regardless of self-esteem levels. The researchers also found that relationship social comparisons were also strongly related to overall relationship satisfaction, investment, and commitment levels. Insecurity also appeared to mediate those relationships.

4. **Perceptions of embarrassing events**: *Do we experience embarrassment for others, even when we are not threatened?*

Miller (1987) proposed and showed that people experience empathy in response to another person's plight, even when there is little chance that they themselves will be embarrassed. They also found that some people are more likely to be embarrassed than others, and these individuals experience more empathy for other persons.

5. **Are you less likely to help others when you are "out of energy?"** *It depends in part on whom you are helping.*

DeWall and colleagues (2008) believed that people are often faced with conflict between the motivation to help others and selfish impulses to not help. In a series of three experiments, they found that when people were depleted of energy to self-regulate, they were less likely (or willing) to help others. In one experiment, they found this to be particularly true when helping strangers, but not true when the person was a family member.

6. **Situational norms**: *Can your environment direct your behavior unknowingly?*

Aarts and Dijksterhuis (2003) hypothesized that environments such as a library setting can automatically trigger norms associated with them (e.g., *Be quiet!*), and these norms automatically make people comply with them. in this research, they showed people photographs of a library or an empty railway station, told some of them that they would be going to those places, and then measured the volume of their voices. As hypothesized, when participants anticipated being in a place where they are expected to be quiet (libraries, fancy restaurants), people automatically adjusted their behaviors in line with the norms of those environments.

7. **Stereotype threat**: *Do people end up confirming stereotypes about their groups when those stereotypes are made salient prior to completing a specific task?*

Beilock, Jellison, Rydell, McConnell, and Carr (2006) asked men who were experts at golf to perform a putting task; however, half of the men were told that "women actually tend to perform better than men on our putting task," whereas the other half were simply told that the putting task is a measure of individual performance. The men who were told that their gender group is not as good at the putting task ended up performing worse than the men who were given no such information.

8. **What do men and women want in a romantic partner?** *It depends upon the social role they envision fulfilling in the future.*

Eagly, Eastwick, and Johannesen-Schmidt (2009) asked male and female college students to imagine themselves in a marital relationship in which they were either in the role of provider or homemaker. Afterward, participants were asked to rate the characteristics desired in a potential mate. In general, imagining oneself as a homemaker resulted in a stronger preference for a partner who was older, career-driven, and wealthier; in contrast, those who imagined themselves as providers wanted partners who were younger, good with children, and competent at cooking and housekeeping.

Review of Key Terms

This course assumes students have at least some prior knowledge of the research process in psychology, either from having taken a general methodology course or from having covered similar information in other psychology courses. As a result, all of the terms that appear below should sound familiar to you. They are provided here as a reference point, because we will use them repeatedly throughout the semester. If you are not familiar with the information on this page, we encourage you to review a basic research methods textbook in order to get comfortable with these terms.

1. **Hypothesis**: A hypothesis is basically a prediction or educated guess about what you think will happen in your study. It specifies the association you expect to find between your independent and dependent variables. It is important that any hypothesis you develop is testable. That is, you must be able to design a study whereby you can gather evidence either for or against it. An example of a testable hypothesis is as follows: "People act more aggressively after playing a violent video game than they do after playing a non-violent game."

2. **Independent Variable (IV)**: The IV is the variable manipulated during an experiment that serves as the cause of any changes in the dependent variable. There are at least two levels or conditions of an IV, but there could be many more depending upon how complex your study is. For example, if you conducted a study to test the hypothesis mentioned above, the IV would be exposure to video game violence because you expect this to affect how aggressively people will act. As the researcher, you will therefore manipulate how much exposure to violence participants will receive (i.e., a lot or a little). One last note about IVs: sometimes they cannot be manipulated because it is not possible or ethical to do so (e.g., someone's personality characteristics or relationship status). In these cases, we simply record the IV through survey or observation and see if it is correlated or associated with the dependent variable. Keep in mind, however, that correlational studies prevent us from making claims about cause-and-effect.

3. **Dependent Variable (DV)**: The DV is the variable that is measured or observed during the course of the experiment. It is the variable we expect to change as a result of participants' exposure to differing levels of the IV (in other words, the DV is *dependent* upon the IV). In our hypothetical study of video game violence and aggression, the DV would be the participants' aggressive tendencies observed after playing the game.

4. **Operationalization**: This refers to the process of putting your IV and DV into very specific,

testable terms. For example, in our video game violence study, you need to clarify what you mean by "exposure to video game violence" and "aggressive tendencies," because these are pretty vague. Thus, you might operationalize your IV as five minutes of playing the most recent *Call of Duty* game (high violence) vs. five minutes of playing Wii Fit (low violence), whereas you might operationalize your DV as the amount of hot sauce a participant pours into a glass for another person to drink (this is actually a common way of measuring how aggressive people feel—although keep in mind that nobody actually drinks the hot sauce. That would just be cruel!).

5. **Random Assignment to Conditions**: In any given experiment, participants should be randomly assigned to conditions. In other words, each participant should have an equal chance of receiving each level of the IV. This can be implemented any number of ways (e.g., using a computerized random number generator, pulling numbers out of a hat, etc.). It does not matter exactly how you do it, as long as it is performed. What this does is ensure that the participant makeup across conditions is as equivalent as possible (i.e., that you have approximately equal numbers of men and women, Democrats and Republicans, etc. receiving each level of the IV). If you do not perform random assignment, you cannot know for sure whether your IV was truly responsible for any changes that occurred in the DV. For example, in our video game violence study, if you simply let participants pick which game they prefer to play, you might end up with mostly men playing the violent game, and mostly women playing the non-violent game. Although you might find that those who played the violent game were more aggressive afterwards, you would not know whether this was caused by the game itself, or if it is because those who played the game were mostly men, and men tend to be more aggressive in general.

6. **Random Selection**: Random selection occurs when everyone in your *target population* (i.e., the overall group of people you are interested in studying) has an equal chance of being selected for inclusion in your study. There are many ways to accomplish this (e.g., if you were interested in studying the effects of video game violence on students at your University, you could get the e-mail list for all students at your school and have

a computer program randomly select 100 of them for you to contact). However, for most psychological studies, including the one you will carry out in this course, this is often not possible or practical. Random selection is typically expensive and difficult to employ, and even when attempted, it is not always perfect because not everyone you select will want to participate in your study. Thus, researchers often choose a *convenience sample* instead (i.e., a group of people that is easy to access for a given study, but that does not necessarily represent the target population).

A word of caution going forward: Keep in mind the differences between random selection and random assignment, because students frequently confuse them in their papers!

Lab #1

Purpose:

- This first lab is designed to give you an overview of the course and what will be expected.
- You will have a chance to get to know the other students in the lab.

Objectives:

- Review the course objectives, requirements, and schedule.
- Do the icebreaker activity to get to know your classmates.

Homework:

- Soak it all in and decide whether you can meet the course requirements.
- Review the key terms on the preceding two pages to ensure that you are up to speed on the necessary background information.
- Read the Baumrind and Milgram articles.

ETHICAL ISSUES IN SOCIAL PSYCHOLOGY RESEARCH

Some Thoughts on Ethics of Research

After Reading Milgram's "Behavioral Study of Obedience"

By Diana Baumrind

CERTAIN problems in psychological research require the experimenter to balance his career and scientific interests against the interests of his prospective subjects. When such occasions arise the experimenter's stated objective frequently is to do the best possible job with the least possible harm to his subjects. The experimenter seldom perceives in more positive terms an indebtedness to the subject for his services, perhaps because the detachment which his functions require prevents appreciation of the subject as an individual.

Yet a debt does exist, even when the subject's reason for volunteering includes course credit or monetary gain. Often a subject participates unwillingly in order to satisfy a course requirement. These requirements are of questionable merit ethically, and do not alter the experimenter's responsibility to the subject.

Most experimental conditions do not cause the subjects pain or indignity, and are sufficiently interesting or challenging to present no problem of an ethical nature to the experimenter. But where the experimental conditions expose the subject to loss of dignity, or offer him nothing of value, then the experimenter is obliged to consider the reasons why the subject volunteered and to reward him accordingly.

The subject's public motives for volunteering include having an enjoyable or stimulating experience, acquiring knowledge, doing the experimenter a favor which may some day be reciprocated, and making a contribution to science. These motives can be taken into account rather easily by the experimenter who is willing to spend a few minutes with the subject afterwards to thank him for his participation, answer his questions, reassure him that he did well, and chat with him a bit. Most volunteers also have less manifest, but equally legitimate, motives. A subject may be seeking an opportunity to have contact with, be noticed by, and perhaps confide in a person with psychological training. The dependent attitude of most subjects toward the experimenter is an artifact of the experimental situation as well as an expression of some subjects' personal need systems at the time they volunteer.

The dependent, obedient attitude assumed by most subjects in the experimental setting is appropriate to that situation. The "game" is defined by the experimenter and he makes the rules. By volunteering, the subject agrees implicitly to assume a posture of trust and obedience. While the experimental conditions leave him exposed, the subject has the right to assume that his security and self-esteem will be protected.

There are other professional situations in which one member—the patient or client—expects help and protection from the other—the physician or psychologist. But the interpersonal relationship between experimenter and subject additionally has unique features which are likely

Diana Baumrind, "Some Thoughts on Ethics of Research: After Reading Milgram's 'Behavioral Study of Obedience'," *American Psychologist*, vol. 19, no. 6, pp. 421–423. Copyright © 1964 by American Psychological Association. Reprinted with permission.

to provoke initial anxiety in the subject. The laboratory is unfamiliar as a setting and the rules of behavior ambiguous compared to a clinician's office. Because of the anxiety and passivity generated by the setting, the subject is more prone to behave in an obedient, suggestible manner in the laboratory than elsewhere. Therefore, the laboratory is not the place to study degree of obedience or suggestibility, as a function of a particular experimental condition, since the base line for these phenomena as found in the laboratory is probably much higher than in most other settings. Thus experiments in which the relationship to the experimenter as an authority is used as an independent condition are imperfectly designed for the same reason that they are prone to injure the subjects involved. They disregard the special quality of trust and obedience with which the subject appropriately regards the experimenter.

Other phenomena which present ethical decisions, unlike those mentioned above, can be reproduced successfully in the laboratory. Failure experience, conformity to peer judgment, and isolation are among such phenomena. In these cases we can expect the experimenter to take whatever measures are necessary to prevent the subject from leaving the laboratory more humiliated, insecure, alienated, or hostile than when he arrived. To guarantee that an especially sentisitive subject leaves a stressful experimental experience in the proper state sometimes requires special clinical training. But usually an attitude of compassion, respect, gratitude, and common sense will suffice, and no amount of clinical training will substitute. The subject has the right to expect that the psychologist with whom he is interacting has some concern for his welfare, and the personal attributes and professional skill to express his good will effectively.

Unfortunately, the subject is not always treated with the respect he deserves. It has become more commonplace in sociopsychological laboratory studies to manipulate, embarrass, and discomfort subjects. At times the insult to the subject's sensibilities extends to the journal reader when the results are reported. Milgram's (1963) study is a case in point. The following is Milgram's abstract of his experiment:

This article describes a procedure for the study of destructive obedience in the laboratory. It consists of ordering a naive S to administer increasingly more severe punishment to a victim in the context of a learning experiment. Punishment is administered by means of a shock generator with 30 graded switches ranging from Slight Shock to Danger: Severe Shock. The victim is a confederate of E. The primary dependent variable is the maximum shock the S is willing to administer before he refuses to continue further. 26 Ss obeyed the experimental commands fully, and administered the highest shock on the generator. 14 Ss broke off the experiment at some point after the victim protested and refused to provide further answers. The procedure created extreme levels of nervous tension in some Ss. Profuse sweating, trembling, and stuttering were typical expressions of this emotional disturbance. One unexpected sign of tension—yet to be explained—was the regular occurrence of nervous laughter, which in some Ss developed into uncontrollable seizures. The variety of interesting behavioral dynamics observed in the experiment, the reality of the situation for the S, and the possibility of parametric variation within the framework of the procedure, point to the fruitfulness of further study [p. 371].

The detached, objective manner in which Milgram reports the emotional disturbance suffered by his subject contrasts sharply with his graphic account of that disturbance. Following are two other quotes describing the effects on his subjects of the experimental conditions :

I observed a mature and initially poised businessman enter the laboratory smiling and confident. Within 20 minutes he was reduced to a twitching, stuttering wreck, who was rapidly approaching a point of nervous collapse. He constantly pulled on his earlobe, and twisted his hands. At one point he pushed his fist into his forehead and muttered: "Oh God, let's stop it." And yet he continued to respond to every word of the experimenter, and obeyed to the end [p. 377].

In a large number of cases the degree of tension reached extremes that are rarely seen in sociopsychological laboratory studies. Subjects were observed to sweat, tremble, stutter, bite their lips, groan, and dig their fingernails into their flesh. These were characteristic rather than exceptional responses to the experiment.

One sign of tension was the regular occurrence of nervous laughing fits. Fourteen of the 40 subjects showed definite signs of nervous laughter and smiling. The laughter seemed entirely out of place, even bizarre. Full-blown, uncontrollable seizures were observed for 3 subjects. On one occasion we observed a seizure so violently convulsive that it was necessary to call a halt to the experiment … [p. 375].

Milgram does state that,

After the interview, procedures were undertaken to assure that the subject would leave the laboratory in a state of well being. A friendly reconciliation was arranged between the subject and the victim, and an effort was made to reduce any tensions that arose as a result of the experiment [p. 374].

It would be interesting to know what sort of procedures could dissipate the type of emotional disturbance just described. In view of the effects on subjects, traumatic to a degree which Milgram himself considers nearly unprecedented in sociopsychological experiments, his casual assurance that these tensions were dissipated before the subject left the laboratory is unconvincing.

What could be the rational basis for such a posture of indifference? Perhaps Milgram supplies the answer himself when he partially explains the subject's destructive obedience as follows, "Thus they assume that the discomfort caused the victim is momentary, while the scientific gains resulting from the experiment are enduring [p. 378]." Indeed such a rationale might suffice to justify the means used to achieve his end if that end were of inestimable value to humanity or were not itself transformed by the means by which it was attained.

The behavioral psychologist is not in as good a position to objectify his faith in the significance of his work as medical colleagues at points of breakthrough. His experimental situations are not sufficiently accurate models of real-life experience; his sampling techniques are seldom of a scope which would justify the meaning with which he would like to endow his results; and these results are hard to reproduce by colleagues with opposing theoretical views. Unlike the Sabin vaccine, for example, the concrete benefit to humanity of his particular piece of work, no matter how competently handled, cannot justify the risk that real harm will be done to the subject. I am not speaking of physical discomfort, inconvenience, or experimental deception per se, but of permanent harm, however slight. I do regard the emotional disturbance described by Milgram as potentially harmful because it could easily effect an alteration in the subject's self-image or ability to trust adult authorities in the future. It is potentially harmful to a subject to commit, in the course of an experiment, acts which he himself considers unworthy, particularly when he has been entrapped into committing such acts by an individual he has reason to trust. The subject's personal responsibility for his actions is not erased because the experimenter reveals to him the means which he used to stimulate these actions. The subject realizes that he would have hurt the victim if the current were on. The realization that he also made a fool of himself by accepting the experimental set results in additional loss of self-esteem. Moreover, the subject finds it difficult to express his anger outwardly after the experimenter in a self-acceptant but friendly manner reveals the hoax.

A fairly intense corrective interpersonal experience is indicated wherein the subject admits and accepts his responsibility for his own actions, and at the same time gives vent to his hurt and anger at being fooled. Perhaps an experience as distressing as the one described by Milgram can be integrated by the subject, provided that careful thought is given to the matter. The propriety of such experimentation is still in question even if such a reparational experience were forthcoming. Without it I would expect a naive, sensitive subject to remain deeply hurt and anxious for some time, and a sophisticated, cynical subject to become even more alienated and distrustful.

In addition the experimental procedure used by Milgram does not appear suited to the objectives of the study because it does not take into account the special quality of the set which the subject has in the experimental situation. Milgram is concerned with a very important problem, namely, the social consequences of destructive obedience. He says,

> Gas chambers were built, death camps were guarded, daily quotas of corpses were produced with the same efficiency as the manufacture of appliances. These inhumane policies may have originated in the mind of a single person, but they could only be carried out on a massive scale if a very large number of persons obeyed orders [p. 371].

But the parallel between authority-subordinate relationships in Hitler's Germany and in Milgram's laboratory is unclear. In the former situation the SS man or member of the German Officer Corps, when obeying orders to slaughter, had no reason to think of his superior officer as benignly disposed towards himself or their

victims. The victims were perceived as subhuman and not worthy of consideration. The subordinate officer was an agent in a great cause. He did not need to feel guilt or conflict because within his frame of reference he was acting rightly.

It is obvious from Milgram's own descriptions that most of his subjects were concerned about their victims and did trust the experimenter, and that their distressful conflict was generated in part by the consequences of these two disparate but appropriate attitudes. Their distress may have resulted from shock at what the experimenter was doing to them as well as from what they thought they were doing to their victims. In any case there is not a convincing parallel between the phenomena studied by Milgram and destructive obedience as that concept would apply to the subordinate-authority relationship demonstrated in Hitler Germany. If the experiments were conducted "outside of New Haven and without any visible ties to the university," I would still question their validity on similar although not identical grounds. In addition, I would question the representativeness of a sample of subjects who would voluntarily participate within a noninstitutional setting.

In summary, the experimental objectives of the psychologist are seldom incompatible with the subject's ongoing state of well being, provided that the experimenter is willing to take the subject's motives and interests into consideration when planning his methods and correctives. Section 4b in Ethical Standards of Psychologists (APA, undated) reads in part:

> Only when a problem is significant and can be investigated in no other way, is the psychologist justified in exposing human subjects to emotional stress or other possible harm. In conducting such research, the psychologist must seriously consider the possibility of harmful aftereffects, and should be prepared to remove them as soon as permitted by the design of the

experiment. Where the danger of serious aftereffects exists, research should be conducted only when the subjects or their responsible agents are fully informed of this possibility and volunteer nevertheless [p. 12].

From the subject's point of view procedures which involve loss of dignity, self-esteem, and trust in rational authority are probably most harmful in the long run and require the most thoughtfully planned reparations, if engaged in at all. The public image of psychology as a profession is highly related to our own actions, and some of these actions are changeworthy. It is important that as research psychologists we protect our ethical sensibilities rather than adapt our personal standards to include as appropriate the kind of indignities to which Milgram's subjects were exposed. I would not like to see experiments such as Milgram's proceed unless the subjects were fully informed of the dangers of serious aftereffects and his correctives were clearly shown to be effective in restoring their state of well being.

REFERENCES

American Psychological Association. Ethical Standards of Psychologists: A summary of ethical principles. Washington, D. C.: APA, undated.

Milgram, S. Behavioral study of obedience. *J. abnorm. soc. Psychol,* 1963, 67, 371–378.

Issues in the Study of Obedience

A Reply to Baumrind

By Stanley Milgram

OBEDIENCE serves numerous productive functions in society. It may be ennobling and educative and entail acts of charity and kindness. Yet the problem of destructive obedience, because it is the most disturbing expression of obedience in our time, and because it is the most perplexing, merits intensive study.

In its most general terms, the problem of destructive obedience may be defined thus: If X tells Y to hurt Z, under what conditions will Y carry out the command of X, and under what conditions will he refuse? In the concrete setting of a laboratory, the question may assume this form: If an experimenter tells a subject to act against another person, under what conditions will the subject go along with the instruction, and under what conditions will he refuse to obey?

A simple procedure was devised for studying obedience (Milgram, 1963). A person comes to the laboratory, and in the context of a learning experiment, he is told to give increasingly severe electric shocks to another person. (The other person is an actor, who does not really receive any shocks.) The experimenter tells the subject to continue stepping up the shock level, even to the point of reaching the level marked "Danger: Severe Shock." The purpose of the experiment is to see how far the naive subject will proceed before he refuses to comply with the experimenter's instructions. Behavior prior to this rupture is considered "obedience" in that the subject does what the experimenter tells him to do. The point of rupture is the act of disobedience. Once the basic procedure is established, it becomes possible to vary conditions of the experiment, to learn under what circumstances obedience to authority is most probable, and under what conditions defiance is brought to the fore (Milgram, in press).

The results of the experiment (Milgram, 1963) showed, first, that it is more difficult for many people to defy the experimenter's authority than was generally supposed. A substantial number of subjects go through to the end of the shock board. The second finding is that the situation often places a person in considerable conflict. In the course of the experiment, subjects fidget, sweat, and sometimes break out into nervous fits of laughter. On the one hand, subjects want to aid the experimenter; and on the other hand, they do not want to shock the learner. The conflict is expressed in nervous reactions.

In a recent issue of *American Psychologist*, Diana Baumrind (1964) raised a number of questions concerning the obedience report. Baumrind expressed concern for the welfare of subjects who served in the experiment, and wondered whether adequate measures were taken to protect the participants. She also questioned the adequacy of the experimental design.

Patently, "Behavioral Study of Obedience" did not contain all the information needed for an assessment of the experiment. But it is clearly

Stanley Milgram, "Issues in the Study of Obedience: A Reply to Baumrind," *American Psychologist*, vol. 19, no. 11, pp. 848–852. Copyright © 1964 by Alexandra Milgram. Reprinted with permission.

indicated in the references and footnotes (pp. 373, 378) that this was only one of a series of reports on the experimental program, and Baumrind's article was deficient in information that could have been obtained easily. I thank the editor for allotting space in this journal to review this information, to amplify it, and to discuss some of the issues touched on by Baumrind.

At the outset, Baumrind confuses the unanticipated outcome of an experiment with its basic procedure. She writes, for example, as if the production of stress in our subjects was an intended and deliberate effect of the experimental manipulation. There are many laboratory procedures specifically designed to create stress (Lazarus, 1964), but the obedience paradigm was not one of them. The extreme tension induced in some subjects was unexpected. Before conducting the experiment, the procedures were discussed with many colleagues, and none anticipated the reactions that subsequently took place. Foreknowledge of results can never be the invariable accompaniment of an experimental probe. Understanding grows because we examine situations in which the end is unknown. An investigator unwilling to accept this degree of risk must give up the idea of scientific inquiry.

Moreover, there was every reason to expect, prior to actual experimentation, that subjects would refuse to follow the experimenter's instructions beyond the point where the victim protested; many colleagues and psychiatrists were questioned on this point, and they virtually all felt this would be the case. Indeed, to initiate an experiment in which the critical measure hangs on disobedience, one must start with a belief in certain spontaneous resources in men that enable them to overcome pressure from authority.

It is true that after a reasonable number of subjects had been exposed to the procedures, it became evident that some would go to the end of the shock board, and some would experience stress. That point, it seems to me, is the first legitimate juncture at which one could even start to wonder whether or not to abandon the study.

But momentary excitement is not the same as harm. As the experiment progressed there was no indication of injurious effects in the subjects; and as the subjects themselves strongly endorsed the experiment, the judgment I made was to continue the investigation.

Is not Baumrind's criticism based as much on the unanticipated findings as on the method? The findings were that some subjects performed in what appeared to be a shockingly immoral way. If, instead, every one of the subjects had broken off at "slight shock," or at the first sign of the learner's discomfort, the results would have been pleasant, and reassuring, and who would protest?

Procedures and Benefits

A most important aspect of the procedure occurred at the end of the experimental session. A careful post-experimental treatment was administered to all subjects. The exact content of the dehoax varied from condition to condition and with increasing experience on our part. At the very least all subjects were told that the victim had not received dangerous electric shocks. Each subject had a friendly reconciliation with the unharmed victim, and an extended discussion with the experimenter. The experiment was explained to the defiant subjects in a way that supported their decision to disobey the experimenter. Obedient subjects were assured of the fact that their behavior was entirely normal and that their feelings of conflict or tension were shared by other participants. Subjects were told that they would receive a comprehensive report at the conclusion of the experimental series. In some instances, additional detailed and lengthy discussions of the experiments were also carried out with individual subjects.

When the experimental series was complete, subjects received a written report which presented details of the experimental procedure and results. Again their own part in the experiments was treated in a dignified way and their behavior in the experiment respected. All subjects received a follow-up questionnaire regarding their

TABLE 1
Excerpt From Questionnaire Used in a Follow-up Study of the Obedience Research

Now that I have read the report, and all things considered . . .	Defiant	Obedient	All
1. I am very glad to have been in the experiment	40.0%	47.8%	43.5%
2. I am glad to have been in the experiment	43.8%	35.7%	40.2%
3. I am neither sorry nor glad to have been in the experiment	15.3%	14.8%	15.1%
4. I am sorry to have been in the experiment	0.8%	0.7%	0.8%
5. I am very sorry to have been in the experiment	0.0%	1.0%	0.5%

Note—Ninety-two percent of the subjects returned the questionnaire. The characteristics of the nonrespondents were checked against the respondents. They differed from the respondents only with regard to age; younger people were overrepresented in the nonresponding group.

participation in the research, which again allowed expression of thoughts and feelings about their behavior.

The replies to the questionnaire confirmed my impression that participants felt positively toward the experiment. In its quantitative aspect (see Table 1), 84% of the subjects stated they were glad to have been in the experiment; 15% indicated neutral feelings, and 1.3% indicated negative feelings. To be sure, such findings are to be interpreted cautiously, but they cannot be disregarded.

Further, four-fifths of the subjects felt that more experiments of this sort should be carried out, and 74% indicated that they had learned something of personal importance as a result of being in the study. The results of the interviews, questionnaire responses, and actual transcripts of the debriefing procedures will be presented more fully in a forthcoming monograph.

The debriefing and assessment procedures were carried out as a matter of course, and were not stimulated by any observation of special risk in the experimental procedure. In my judgment, at no point were subjects exposed to danger and at no point did they run the risk of injurious effects resulting from participation. If it had been otherwise, the experiment would have been terminated at once.

Baumrind states that, after he has performed in the experiment, the subject cannot justify his behavior and must bear the full brunt of his actions. By and large it does not work this way. The same mechanisms that allow the subject to perform the act, to obey rather than to defy the experimenter, transcend the moment of performance and continue to justify his behavior for him. The same viewpoint the subject takes while performing the actions is the viewpoint from which he later sees his behavior, that is, the perspective of "carrying out the task assigned by the person in authority."

Because the idea of shocking the victim is repugnant, there is a tendency among those who hear of the design to say "people will not do it." When the results are made known, this attitude is expressed as "if they do it they will not be able to live with themselves afterward." These two forms of denying the experimental findings are equally inappropriate misreadings of the facts of human social behavior. Many subjects do, indeed, obey to the end, and there is no indication of injurious effects.

The absence of injury is a minimal condition of experimentation; there can be, however, an important positive side to participation. Baumrind suggests that subjects derived no benefit from being in the obedience study, but this is false. By their statements and actions, subjects indicated that they had learned a good deal, and many felt gratified to have taken part in scientific research they considered to be of significance. A year after his participation one subject wrote:

> This experiment has strengthened my belief that man should avoid harm to

his fellow man even at the risk of violating authority.

Another stated:

> To me, the experiment pointed up … the extent to which each individual should have or discover firm ground on which to base his decisions, no matter how trivial they appear to be. I think people should think more deeply about themselves and their relation to their world and to other people. If this experiment serves to jar people out of complacency, it will have served its end.

These statements are illustrative of a broad array of appreciative and insightful comments by those who participated.

The 5-page report sent to each subject on the completion of the experimental series was specifically designed to enhance the value of his experience. It layed out the broad conception of the experimental program as well as the logic of its design. It described the results of a dozen of the experiments, discussed the causes of tension, and attempted to indicate the possible significance of the experiment. Subjects responded enthusiastically; many indicated a desire to be in further experimental research. This report was sent to all subjects several years ago. The care with which it was prepared does not support Baumrind's assertion that the experimenter was indifferent to the value subjects derived from their participation.

Baumrind's fear is that participants will be alienated from psychological experiments because of the intensity of experience associated with laboratory procedures. My own observation is that subjects more commonly respond with distaste to the "empty" laboratory hour, in which cardboard procedures are employed, and the only possible feeling upon emerging from the laboratory is that one has wasted time in a patently trivial and useless exercise.

The subjects in the obedience experiment, on the whole, felt quite differently about their participation. They viewed the experience as an opportunity to learn something of importance about themselves, and more generally, about the conditions of human action.

A year after the experimental program was completed, I initiated an additional follow-up study. In this connection an impartial medical examiner, experienced in outpatient treatment, interviewed 40 experimental subjects. The examining psychiatrist focused on those subjects he felt would be most likely to have suffered consequences from participation. His aim was to identify possible injurious effects resulting from the experiment. He concluded that, although extreme stress had been experienced by several subjects,

> none was found by this interviewer to show signs of having been harmed by his experience. … Each subject seemed to handle his task [in the experiment] in a manner consistent with well established patterns of behavior. No evidence was found of any traumatic reactions.

Such evidence ought to be weighed before judging the experiment.

Other Issues

Baumrind's discussion is not limited to the treatment of subjects, but diffuses to a generalized rejection of the work.

Baumrind feels that obedience cannot be meaningfully studied in a laboratory setting: The reason she offers is that "The dependent, obedient attitude assumed by most subjects in the experimental setting is appropriate to that situation [p. 421]." Here, Baumrind has cited the very best reason for examining obedience in this setting, namely that it possesses "ecological validity." Here is one social context in which compliance occurs regularly. Military and job situations are also particularly meaningful settings for the study of obedience precisely because obedience is natural and appropriate to these contexts. I reject Baumrind's argument that the observed obedience does not count because it occurred where it is appropriate. That is precisely why it does count. A soldier's obedience is no less meaningful because it occurs in a pertinent military context. A subject's obedience is no less problematical because it occurs within a social institution called the psychological experiment.

Baumrind writes: "The game is defined by the experimenter and he makes the rules [p. 421]." It is true that for disobedience to occur the framework of the experiment must be shattered. That, indeed, is the point of the design. That is why obedience and disobedience are genuine issues for the subject. *He must really assert himself as a person against a legitimate authority.*

Further, Baumrind wants us to believe that outside the laboratory we could not find a comparably high expression of obedience. Yet, the fact that ordinary citizens are recruited to military service and, on command, perform far harsher acts against people is beyond dispute. Few of them know or are concerned with the complex policy issues underlying martial action; fewer still become conscientious objectors. Good soldiers do as they are told, and on both sides of the battle line. However, a debate on whether a higher level of obedience is represented by (a) killing men in the service of one's country, or (b) merely shocking them in the service of Yale science, is largely unprofitable. The real question is: What are the forces underlying obedient action?

Another question raised by Baumrind concerns the degree of parallel between obedience in the laboratory and in Nazi Germany. Obviously, there are enormous differences: Consider the disparity in time scale. The laboratory experiment takes an hour; the Nazi calamity unfolded in the space of a decade. There is a great deal that needs to be said on this issue, and only a few points can be touched on here.

1. In arguing this matter, Baumrind mistakes the background metaphor for the precise subject matter of investigation. The German event was cited to point up a serious problem in the human situation: the potentially destructive effect of obedience. But the best way to tackle the problem of obedience, from a scientific standpoint, is in no way restricted by "what happened exactly" in Germany. What happened exactly can never be duplicated in the laboratory or anywhere else. The real task is to learn more about the general problem of destructive obedience using a workable approach. Hopefully, such inquiry will stimulate insights and yield general propositions that can be applied to a wide variety of situations.

2. One may ask in a general way: How does a man behave when he is told by a legitimate authority to act against a third individual? In trying to find an answer to this question, the laboratory situation is one useful starting point—and for the very reason stated by Baumrind—namely, the experimenter does constitute a genuine authority for the subject. The fact that trust and dependence on the experimenter are maintained, despite the extraordinary harshness he displays toward the victim, is itself a remarkable phenomenon.

3. In the laboratory, through a set of rather simple manipulations, ordinary persons no longer perceived themselves as a responsible part of the causal chain leading to action against a person. The means through which responsibility is cast off, and individuals become thoughtless agents of action, is of general import. Other processes were revealed that indicate that the experiments will help us to understand why men obey. That understanding will come, of course, by examining the full account of experimental work and not alone the brief report in which the procedure and demonstrational results were exposed.

At root, Baumrind senses that it is not proper to test obedience in this situation, because she construes it as one in which there is no reasonable alternative to obedience. In adopting this view, she has lost sight of this fact: A substantial proportion of subjects do disobey. By their example, disobedience is shown to be a genuine possibility, one that is in no sense ruled out by the general structure of the experimental situation.

Baumrind is uncomfortable with the high level of obedience obtained in the first experiment. In the condition she focused on, 65% of the subjects obeyed to the end. However, her sentiment does not take into account that within the general framework of the psychological experiment obedience varied enormously from one condition to the next. In some variations, 90% of the subjects disobeyed. It seems to be not only the fact of an experiment, but the particular structure of elements within the experimental situation that accounts for rates of obedience and disobedience. And these elements were varied systematically in the program of research.

A concern with human dignity is based on a respect for a man's potential to act morally. Baumrind feels that the experimenter made the subject shock the victim. This conception is alien to my view. The experimenter tells the subject to do something. But between the command and the outcome there is a paramount force, the acting person who may obey or disobey. I started with the belief that every person who came to the laboratory was free to accept or to reject the dictates of authority. This view sustains a conception of human dignity insofar as it sees in each man a capacity for choosing his own behavior. And as it turned out, many subjects did, indeed, choose to reject the experimenter's commands, providing a powerful affirmation of human ideals.

Baumrind also criticizes the experiment on the grounds that "it could easily effect an alteration in the subject's . . . ability to trust adult authorities in the future [p. 422]." But I do not think she can have it both ways. On the one hand, she argues the experimental situation is so special that it has no generality; on the other hand, she states it has such generalizing potential that it will cause subjects to distrust all authority. But the experimenter is not just any authority: He is an authority who tells the subject to act harshly and inhumanely against another man. I would

consider it of the highest value if participation in the experiment could, indeed, inculcate a skepticism of this kind of authority. Here, perhaps, a difference in philosophy emerges most clearly. Baumrind sees the subject as a passive creature, completely controlled by the experimenter. I started from a different viewpoint. A person who comes to the laboratory is an active, choosing adult, capable of accepting or rejecting the prescriptions for action addressed to him. Baumrind sees the effect of the experiment as undermining the subject's trust of authority. I see it as a potentially valuable experience insofar as it makes people aware of the problem of indiscriminate submission to authority.

Conclusion

My feeling is that viewed in the total context of values served by the experiment, approximately the right course was followed. In review, the facts are these: (a) At the outset, there was the problem of studying obedience by means of a simple experimental procedure. The results could not be foreseen before the experiment was carried out. (6) Although the experiment generated momentary stress in some subjects, this stress dissipated quickly and was not injurious. (c) Dehoax and follow-up procedures were carried out to insure the subjects' well-being. (d) These procedures were assessed through questionnaire and psychiatric studies and were found to be effective. (e) Additional steps were taken to enhance the value of the laboratory experience for participants, for example, submitting to each subject a careful report on the experimental program. (f) The subjects themselves strongly endorse the experiment, and indicate satisfaction at having participated.

If there is a moral to be learned from the obedience study, it is that every man must be responsible for his own actions. This author accepts full responsibility for the design and execution of the study. Some people may feel it should not have been done. I disagree and accept the burden of their judgment.

Baumrind's judgment, someone has said, not only represents a personal conviction, but also reflects a cleavage in American psychology between those whose primary concern is with helping people and those who are interested mainly in learning about people. I see little value in perpetuating divisive forces in psychology when there is so much to learn from every side. A schism may exist, but it does not correspond to the true ideals of the discipline. The psychologist intent on healing knows that his power to help rests on knowledge; he is aware that a scientific grasp of all aspects of life is essential for his work, and is in itself a worthy human aspiration. At the same time, the laboratory psychologist senses his work will lead to human betterment, not only because enlightenment is more dignified than ignorance, but because new knowledge is pregnant with humane consequences.

REFERENCES

BAUMRIND, D. Some thoughts on ethics of research: After reading Milgram's "Behavioral study of obedience." *Amer. Psychologist,* 1964, 19, 421–423.

LAZARUS, R. A laboratory approach to the dynamics of psychological stress. *Amer. Psychologist,* 1964, 19, 400–411.

MILGRAM, S. Behavioral study of obedience. *J. abnorm. soc. Psychol.,* 1963, 67, 371–378.

MILGRAM, S. Some conditions of obedience and disobedience to authority. *Hum. Relat.,* in press.

Lab #2

Purpose:

- This lab is designed to introduce you to the subject of ethics.

Objectives:

- Review the following section entitled Research Ethics in Social Psychology.
- Discuss the Baumrind and Milgram articles and how they relate to ethics in research.
- Complete the in-class ethical issues exercise.
- Turn in rank ordering of the research paper topics in order of preference.

Homework:

- Read the Jordan and Zanna article.
- Bring your APA publication manual or the APA style guide to the next lab (it is strongly recommended that you purchase your own copy of one of these books, especially if you are planning to go to graduate school in psychology).
- If you are unable to purchase them, you may find the following websites to be helpful throughout the semester:
    - » http://www.apastyle.org/learn/tutorials/basics-tutorial.aspx
        - · This website offers a video tutorial covering all aspects of APA style.
    - » http://owl.english.purdue.edu/owl/resource/560/01/
    - » http://psychology.vanguard.edu/faculty/douglas-degelman/apa-style/
        - · Both of these websites offer handy summaries covering most elements of APA style.

Research Ethics in Social Psychology

Just a few decades ago, psychological research was subject to relatively little oversight. Studies that would be second guessed or prohibited by today's standards could be carried out relatively easily because Institutional Review Boards (IRBs) did not yet exist and there were no federal laws regulating the conduct of research at colleges and universities. Consequently, there are more than a few studies in psychology's past that we now look back on as being ethically questionable. These include Milgram's (1963) studies on obedience to authority, as well as the Stanford Prison Experiment (Haney, Banks, & Zimbardo, 1973). To this day, many psychologists continue to question whether the knowledge we gained from these two studies was worth the psychological distress experienced by participants.

As a result, modern psychological research is scrutinized at a much higher level than ever before and any given study must meet certain ethical requirements before it can be carried out. These requirements are aimed at ensuring that participants' rights are respected and that no harm comes to those who volunteer to take part in our research. To that end, informed consent, debriefing, and confidentiality have become the minimum requirements of almost any given psychological study.

Informed consent means that participants must be notified of their rights, the nature of the study, as well as any potential risks and benefits associated with the study's procedures. Without this information, participants cannot truly make an informed decision as to whether they want to take part in the study. Of course, some amount of **deception** is deemed acceptable in order to ensure the validity of your data (e.g., you do not have to tell participants your hypothesis and all of the details about how you will manipulate your variables); however, you cannot withhold or lie about information that would affect participants' willingness to take part in your study. It is important to note that simply having a cover story to avoid giving away your hypothesis is NOT how social psychologists define deception. For example, if you were to conduct a study in which you predicted that photographs and posts on Facebook about alcohol use could impact perceived norms about alcohol consumption, you could have as your cover story that the study is about how people form impressions of others using social media. This is not deception, because your participants *are* forming impressions of others in your study using the stimuli you provide them, and they can make enough of an informed decision about participating based on this knowledge. Deception would involve telling your participants one thing, but doing something entirely different, such as telling participants that they will be completing a standardized test of their abilities, and then (unknowingly) giving participants false feedback on their performance (e.g., telling them that they performed poorly when they actually did quite well).

Debriefing means that participants must be told the true purpose of the research at the end of the study. In addition, any deception that occurred must be explained. This is to ensure that participants do not leave with any misconceptions or misinformation. Also, if there were any risks to participants (e.g., emotional distress), appropriate resources must be provided. There are only rare instances in which a researcher can argue that debriefing is not possible or that doing so would potentially cause more harm to participants than saying nothing. One situation in which this may be the case is if you designed an observational study. In this case, debriefing might not be feasible or could cause harm to participants if you were to approach them after your observation to notify them that they were being watched and/or their behaviors recorded.

Confidentiality means that research psychologists must protect their participants' private information. This means that you cannot reveal any personally identifying information about your participants to anyone. Confidentiality is vital in psychological research because we often collect very personal information (e.g., experiences with infidelity) that could be damaging if revealed. Also, if we cannot guarantee confidentiality, participants will be less inclined to answer our questions honestly and accurately. We must take many precautions to ensure confidentiality, including how we ask and gather our questions, to how we store our information (e.g., using password protected computers or encrypted data transmission systems).

For the research project you carry out in this course, you will be required to uphold these ethical standards; however, there may be a number of other rules and requirements you must address as well depending upon your instructor and institution. Please be mindful and respectful of these requirements and keep in mind that they do not exist simply to make your life more complicated. Your participants are doing you and the field a valuable service by taking part in your research and, as such, they deserve your respect and protection.

References

Haney, C., Banks, W.C., & Zimbardo, P.G. (1973). Interpersonal dynamics in a simulated prison. *International Journal of Criminology and Penology, 1,* 69–97. doi: 10.1037/h0076835

Milgram, S. (1963). Behavioral study of obedience. *Journal of Abnormal and Social Psychology, 67,* 371–378. doi:10.1037/h0040525

In-Class Ethical Issues Exercise

For this exercise, your instructor will assign each research team to read about one study (the complete citation is included). Based upon the reading and ethics discussion you had, answer the questions following your assigned study's description. For each of them, consider whether the potential findings were important enough (either theoretically or practically) to justify the procedure that was used.

1. Bramel led heterosexual male undergraduates to believe that they were sexually aroused by photographs of other men. Bergin gave participants of both sexes discrepant information about their level of masculinity or femininity (e.g., someone who was masculine might have been told that they were feminine). In one of Bergin's experimental conditions, that information was presumably based upon an elaborate series of psychological tests the participants had taken. In all studies, the deception was explained to the participant at the end of the experiment.

Bramel, D. A. (1962). Dissonance theory approach to defensive projection. *Journal of Abnormal and Social Psychology, 64,* 121–29.

Bramel, D. A., (1963). Selection of a target for defensive projection. *Journal of Abnormal and Social Psychology, 66,* 318–24.

Bergin, A. E. (1962). The effect of dissonant persuasive communication on changes in a self-referring attitude. *Journal of Personality, 30,* 423–38.

What ethical problems do you see in these studies? Was there a danger to the participants' physical or psychological well-being? If so, what was it? Did the participants learn something valuable about themselves?

2. After participants performed a very tedious research task, the investigator made it clear—through words and gestures—that the experiment was over, and that he would now "like to explain what this had been all about so you'll have some idea of why you were doing this." This explanation was false, and was actually the basis for the true experimental manipulation, which involved asking participants to serve as the experimenter's accomplices. The task of each accomplice was to lie and tell a future participant that the experiment was interesting and enjoyable (when, in fact, it was a rather boring experience). He or she was also asked to be on call for unspecified future occasions when his or her services as an accomplice might be needed, in case their regular person could not make it. These newly recruited accomplices were, of course, the true participants, while the "participants" who were being lied to were actors (sometimes called "confederates") and knew what was really going on. For serving as an accomplice, the true participants were paid in advance. Half of them received $1; the other half, $20. However, when they completed their tasks, the investigators asked them to return the money.

Festinger, L., & Carlsmith, J. M. (1959). Cognitive consequences of forced compliance. *Journal of Abnormal and Social Psychology, 58,* 203–10.

What are the ethical problems raised by the study? Was the dignity or privacy of the participants endangered? If so, how? What did the participants gain from taking part in the study?

3. Housewives are phoned. The caller claims to represent a fictitious consumer's group, and interviews them about the soap products they use for a report in a "public service publication," which is also given a fictitious name. Several days later, the experimenter calls again, and asks if the housewives would allow five or six men into their homes to "enumerate and classify" all of their household products for another report in the same publication. If the housewife agrees, the caller says he is just collecting names of willing people at present, and that she will be contacted if they decide to use her in the survey. No one is contacted again.

Freedman, J. L., & Fraser, S. C. (1966). Compliance without pressure: The foot-in-the-door technique. *Journal of Personality and Social Psychology, 4,* 195–202.

What are the ethical issues raised by this field experiment? Do phone calls constitute an unethical invasion of privacy, or were they no different from other unsolicited calls that people receive from poll takers, salespeople, fund-raisers, et al?

4. A person walking with a cane pretends to collapse in a subway car. "Stage blood" trickles from his mouth. If someone approaches the victim, he allows that person to help him to his feet. If no one approaches him before the train slows to a stop, another researcher, posing as a passenger, pretends to help and both leave the train.

Piliavin, J. A., & Piliavin, I. M. (1972). Effect of blood on reactions to a victim. *Journal of Personality and Social Psychology, 23,* 353–61.

What are the ethical issues raised by this field experiment? Are there any problems with the fact that the subway passengers were unaware that they were participants in a research study? What about the fact that the passengers were engaging in public responses (which could be viewed by many people), and that their responses were not necessarily anonymous?

Research Project Preference

Name: _____

Please rank order the following topics (1 being most preferred, 6 being least preferred) for the research project you will work on this semester. Be sure to assign every topic a number. You will be assigned to a research team based on shared interests, and we will do our best to place you in one of your top choices.

_____ Expression of prejudice: *Are people more likely to express prejudice when their past behavior has established that they are nonprejudiced persons?*

_____ Terror management: *Does thinking about one's own death increase the need to believe that others share your worldview?*

_____ Attachment style and relationship social comparisons: *Are anxious or avoidant people more likely to make relationship comparisons?*

_____ Perceptions of embarrassing events: *Do we experience embarrassment for others, even when we are not threatened?*

_____ Are you less likely to help others when you are "out of energy"? *It depends in part on whom you are helping.*

_____ Situational norms: *Can your environment direct your behavior unknowingly?*

_____ Stereotype threat: *Do people end up confirming stereotypes about their groups when those stereotypes are made salient prior to completing a specific task?*

_____ What do men and women want in a romantic partner? : *It depends on the social role they envision fulfilling in the future.*

UNDERSTANDING AND SUMMARIZING RESEARCH ARTICLES AND APA FORMATTING

How to Read a Journal Article in Social Psychology

By Christian H. Jordan and Mark P. Zanna

W HEN approaching a journal article for the first time, and often on subsequent occasions, most people try to digest it as they would any piece of prose. They start at the beginning and read word for word, until eventually they arrive at the end, perhaps a little bewildered, but with a vague sense of relief. This is not an altogether terrible strategy; journal articles do have a logical structure that lends itself to this sort of reading. There are, however, more efficient approaches that enable you, a student of social psychology, to cut through peripheral details, avoid sophisticated statistics with which you may not be familiar, and focus on the central ideas in an article. Arming yourself with a little foreknowledge of what is contained in journal articles, as well as some practical advice on how to read them, should help you read journal articles more effectively. If this sounds tempting, read on.

Journal articles offer a window into the inner workings of social psychology. They document how social psychologists formulate hypotheses, design empirical studies, analyze the observations they collect, and interpret their results. Journal articles also serve an invaluable archival function: They contain the full store of common and cumulative knowledge of social psychology. Having documentation of past research allows researchers to build on past findings and advance our understanding of social behavior, without pursuing avenues of investigation that have already been explored. Perhaps most importantly, a research study is never complete until its results have been shared with others, colleagues and students alike. Journal articles are a primary means of communicating research findings. As such, they can be genuinely exciting and interesting to read.

That last claim may have caught you off guard. For beginning readers, journal articles may seem anything but interesting and exciting. They may, on the contrary, appear daunting and esoteric, laden with jargon and obscured by menacing statistics. Recognizing this fact, we hope to arm you, through this paper, with the basic information you will need to read journal articles with a greater sense of comfort and perspective. Social psychologists study many fascinating topics, ranging from prejudice and discrimination, to culture, persuasion, liking and love, conformity and obedience, aggression, and the self. In our daily lives, these are issues we often struggle to understand. Social psychologists present systematic observations of, as well as a wealth of ideas about, such issues in journal articles. It would be a shame if the fascination and intrigue these topics have were lost in their translation into journal publications. We don't think they are, and by the end of this paper, hopefully you won't either.

Journal articles come in a variety of forms, including research reports, review articles, and theoretical articles. Put briefly, a research report is a formal presentation of an original research study, or series of studies. A review article is an evaluative survey of previously published work, usually organized by a guiding theory or point of view. The author of a review article summarizes previous investigations of a circumscribed problem, comments on what progress has been made toward its resolution, and suggests areas of the problem that require further study. A theoretical article also evaluates past research, but focuses on the development of theories used to explain empirical findings. Here, the author may present a new theory to explain a set of findings, or may compare and contrast a set of competing theories, suggesting why one theory might be the superior one.

This paper focuses primarily on how to read research reports, for several reasons. First, the bulk of published literature in social psychology consists of research reports. Second, the summaries presented in review articles, and the ideas set forth in theoretical articles, are built on findings presented in research reports. To get a deep understanding of how research is done in social psychology, fluency in reading original research reports is essential. Moreover, theoretical articles frequently report new studies that pit one theory against another, or test a novel prediction derived from a new theory. In order to appraise the validity of such theoretical contentions, a grounded understanding of basic findings is invaluable. Finally, most research reports are written in a standard format that is likely unfamiliar to new readers. The format of review and theoretical articles is less standardized, and more like that of textbooks and other scholarly writings, with which most readers are familiar. This is not to suggest that such articles are easier to read and comprehend than research reports; they can be quite challenging indeed. It is simply the case that, because more rules apply to the writing of research reports, more guidelines can be offered on how to read them.

The Anatomy of Research Reports

Most research reports in social psychology, and in psychology in general, are written in a standard format prescribed by the American Psychological Association (1994). This is a great boon to both readers and writers. It allows writers to present their ideas and findings in a clear, systematic manner. Consequently, as a reader, once you understand this format, you will not be on completely foreign ground when you approach a new research report—regardless of its specific content. You will know where in the paper particular information is found, making it easier to locate. No matter what your reasons for reading a research report, a firm understanding of the format in which they are written will ease your task. We discuss the format of research reports next, with some practical suggestions on how to read them. Later, we discuss how this format reflects the process of scientific investigation, illustrating how research reports have a coherent narrative structure.

Title and Abstract

Though you can't judge a book by its cover, you can learn a lot about a research report simply by reading its title. The title presents a concise statement of the theoretical issues investigated, and/or the variables that were studied. For example, the following title was taken almost at random from a prestigious journal in social psychology: "Sad and guilty? Affective influences on the explanation of conflict in close relationships" (Forgas, 1994, p. 56).

Just by reading the title, it can be inferred that the study investigated how emotional states change the way people explain conflict in close relationships. It also suggests that when feeling sad, people accept more personal blame for such conflicts (i.e., feel more guilty).

The abstract is also an invaluable source of information. It is a brief synopsis of the study, and packs a lot of information into 150 words or less. The abstract contains information about the problem that was investigated, how it was investigated, the major findings of the study, and hints at the theoretical and practical implications of the findings. Thus, the abstract is a useful summary of the research that provides the gist of the investigation. Reading this outline first can be very helpful, because it tells you where the report is going, and gives you a useful framework for organizing information contained in the article.

The title and abstract of a research report are like a movie preview. A movie preview highlights the important aspects of a movie's plot, and provides just enough information for one to decide whether to watch the whole movie. Just so with titles and abstracts; they highlight the key features of a research report to allow you to decide if you want to read the whole paper. And just as with movie previews, they do not give the whole story. Reading just the title and abstract is never enough to fully understand a research report.

Introduction

A research report has four main sections: introduction, method, results, and discussion. Though it is not explicitly labeled, the introduction begins the main body of a research report. Here, the researchers set the stage for the study. They present the problem under investigation, and state why it was important to study. By providing a brief review of past research and theory relevant to the central issue of investigation, the researchers place the study in an historical context and suggest how the study advances knowledge of the problem. Beginning with broad theoretical and practical considerations, the researchers delineate the rationale that led them to the specific set of hypotheses tested in the study. They also describe how they decided on their research strategy (e.g., why they chose an experiment or a correlational study).

The introduction generally begins with a broad consideration of the problem investigated.

Here, the researchers want to illustrate that the problem they studied is a real problem about which people should care. If the researchers are studying prejudice, they may cite statistics that suggest discrimination is prevalent, or describe specific cases of discrimination. Such information helps illustrate why the research is both practically and theoretically meaningful, and why you should bother reading about it. Such discussions are often quite interesting and useful. They can help you decide for yourself if the research has merit. But they may not be essential for understanding the study at hand. Read the introduction carefully, but choose judiciously what to focus on and remember. To understand a study, what you really need to understand is what the researchers' hypotheses were, and how they were derived from theory, informal observation, or intuition. Other background information may be intriguing, but may not be critical to understand what the researchers did and why they did it.

While reading the introduction, try answering these questions: What problem was studied, and why? How does this study relate to, and go beyond, past investigations of the problem? How did the researchers derive their hypotheses? What questions do the researchers hope to answer with this study?

Method

In the method section, the researchers translate their hypotheses into a set of specific, testable questions. Here, the researchers introduce the main characters of the study the subjects or participants- describing their characteristics (gender, age, etc.) and how many of them were involved. Then, they describe the materials (or apparatus), such as any questionnaires or special equipment, used in the study. Finally, they describe chronologically the procedures of the study; that is, how the study was conducted. Often, an overview of the research design will begin the method section.

This overview provides a broad outline of the design, alerting you to what you should attend.

The method is presented in great detail so that other researchers can recreate the study to confirm (or question) its results. This degree of detail is normally not necessary to under- stand a study, so don't get bogged down trying to memorize the particulars of the procedures. Focus on how the independent variables were manipulated (or measured) and how the dependent variables were measured.

Measuring variables adequately is not always an easy matter. Many of the variables psychologists are interested in cannot be directly observed, so they must be inferred from participants' behavior. Happiness, for example, cannot be directly observed. Thus, researchers interested in how being happy influences people's judgments must infer happiness (or its absence) from their behavior—perhaps by asking people how happy they are, and judging their degree of happiness from their responses; perhaps by studying people's facial expressions for signs of happiness, such as smiling. Think about the measures researchers use while reading the method section. Do they adequately reflect or capture the concepts they are meant to measure? If a measure seems odd, consider carefully how the researchers justify its use.

Oftentimes in social psychology, getting there is half the fun. In other words, how a result is obtained can be just as interesting as the result itself. Social psychologists often strive to have participants behave in a natural, spontaneous manner, while controlling enough of their environment to pinpoint the causes of their behavior. Sometimes, the major contribution of a research report is its presentation of a novel method of investigation. When this is the case, the method will be discussed in some detail in the introduction.

Participants in social psychology studies are intelligent and inquisitive people who are responsive to what happens around them. Because of this, they are not always initially told the true purpose of a study. If they were told, they might not act naturally. Thus, researchers frequently need to be creative, presenting a credible rationale for complying with procedures, without revealing the study's purpose. This rationale is known as a cover story, and is often an elaborate scenario. While reading the method section, try putting yourself in the shoes of a participant in the study, and ask yourself if the instructions given to participants seem sensible, realistic, and engaging. Imagining what it was like to be in the study will also help you remember the study's procedure, and aid you in interpreting the study's results.

While reading the method section, try answering these questions: How were the hypotheses translated into testable questions? How were the variables of interest manipulated and/ or measured? Did the measures used adequately reflect the variables of interest? For example, is self-reported income an adequate measure of social class? Why or why not?

Results

The results section describes how the observations collected were analyzed to determine whether the original hypotheses were supported. Here, the data (observations of behavior) are described, and statistical tests are presented. Because of this, the results section is often intimidating to readers who have little or no training in statistics. Wading through complex and unfamiliar statistical analyses is understandably confusing and frustrating. As a result, many students are tempted to skip over reading this section. We advise you not to do so. Empirical findings are the foundation of any science and results sections are where such findings are presented.

Take heart. Even the most prestigious researchers were once in your shoes and sympathize with you. Though space in psychology journals is limited, researchers try to strike a balance between the need to be clear and the need to be brief in describing their results. In an influential paper on how to write good research reports, Bem (1987) offered this advice to researchers:

> No matter how technical or abstruse your article is in its particulars, intelligent non psychologists with no expertise in statistics or experimental design should be able to comprehend the broad outlines of what you did and why. They should understand in general terms what was learned. (p. 74)

Generally speaking, social psychologists try to practice this advice.

Most statistical analyses presented in research reports test specific hypotheses. Often, each analysis presented is preceded by a reminder of the hypothesis it is meant to test. After an analysis is presented, researchers usually provide a narrative description of the result in plain English. When the hypothesis tested by a statistical analysis is not explicitly stated, you can usually determine the hypothesis that was tested by reading this narrative description of the result, and referring back to the introduction to locate an hypothesis that corresponds to that result. After even the most complex statistical analysis, there will be a written description of what the result means conceptually. Turn your attention to these descriptions. Focus on the conceptual meaning of research findings, not on the mechanics of how they were obtained (unless you're comfortable with statistics).

Aside from statistical tests and narrative descriptions of results, results sections also frequently contain tables and graphs. These are efficient summaries of data. Even if you are not familiar with statistics, look closely at tables and graphs, and pay attention to the means or correlations presented in them. Researchers always include written descriptions of the pertinent aspects of tables and graphs. While reading these descriptions, check the tables and graphs to make sure what the researchers say accurately reflects their data. If they say there was a difference between two groups on a particular dependent measure, look at the means in the table that correspond to those two groups, and see if the means do differ as described. Occasionally, results seem to become stronger in their narrative description than an examination of the data would warrant.

Statistics can be misused. When they are, results are difficult to interpret. Having said this, a lack of statistical knowledge should not make you overly cautious while reading results sections. Though not a perfect antidote, journal articles undergo extensive review by professional researchers before publication. Thus, most misapplications of statistics are caught and corrected before an article is published. So, if you are unfamiliar with statistics, you can be reasonably confident that findings are accurately reported.

While reading the results section, try answering these questions: Did the researchers provide evidence that any independent variable manipulations were effective? For example, if testing for behavioral differences between happy and sad participants, did the researchers demonstrate that one group was in fact happier than the other? What were the major findings of the study? Were the researchers' original hypotheses supported by their observations? If not, look in the discussion section for how the researchers explain the findings that were obtained.

Discussion

The discussion section frequently opens with a summary of what the study found, and an evaluation of whether the findings supported the original hypotheses. Here, the researchers evaluate the theoretical and practical implications of their results. This can be particularly interesting when the results did not work out exactly as the researchers anticipated. When such is the case, consider the researchers' explanations carefully, and see if they seem plausible to you. Often, researchers will also report any aspects of their study that limit their interpretation of its results, and suggest further research that could overcome these limitations to provide a better understanding of the problem under investigation.

Some readers find it useful to read the first few paragraphs of the discussion section before reading any other part of a research report. Like the abstract, these few paragraphs usually contain all of the main ideas of a research report: What the hypotheses were, the major findings and whether they supported the original hypotheses, and how the findings relate to past research and theory. Having this information before reading a research report can guide your reading, allowing you to focus on the specific details you need to complete your understanding of a study. The description of the results, for example, will alert you to the major variables that were studied. If they are unfamiliar to you, you can pay special attention to how they are defined in the introduction, and how they are operationalized in the method section.

After you have finished reading an article, it can also be helpful to reread the first few paragraphs of the discussion and the abstract. As noted, these two passages present highly distilled summaries of the major ideas in a research report. Just as they can help guide your reading of a report, they can also help you consolidate your understanding of a report once you have finished reading it. They provide a check on whether you have understood the main points of a report, and offer a succinct digest of the research in the authors' own words.

While reading the discussion section, try answering these questions: What conclusions can be drawn from the study? What new information does the study provide about the problem under investigation? Does the study help resolve the problem? What are the practical and theoretical implications of the study's findings? Did the results contradict past research findings? If so, how do the researchers explain this discrepancy?

Some Notes on Reports of Multiple Studies

Up to this point, we have implicitly assumed that a research report describes just one study. It is also quite common, however, for a research report to describe a series of studies of the same problem in a single article. When such is the case, each study reported will have the same basic structure (introduction, method, results, and discussion sections) that we have outlined, with the notable exception that sometimes the results and discussion section for each study are combined. Combined "results and discussion" sections contain the same information that separate results and discussion sections normally contain. Sometimes, the authors present all their results first, and only then discuss the implications of these results, just as they would in separate results and discussion sections. Other times, however, the authors alternate between describing results and discussing their implications, as each result is presented. In either case, you should be on the lookout for the same information, as outlined above in our consideration of separate results and discussion sections.

Reports including multiple studies also differ from single study reports in that they include more general introduction and discussion sections. The general introduction, which begins the main body of a research report, is similar in essence to the introduction of a single study report. In both cases, the researchers describe the problem investigated and its practical and theoretical significance. They also demonstrate how they derived their hypotheses, and explain how their research relates to past investigations of the problem. In contrast, the separate introductions to each individual study in reports of multiple studies are usually quite brief, and focus more specifically on the logic and rationale of each particular study presented. Such introductions generally describe the methods used in the particular study, outlining how they answer questions that have not been adequately addressed by past research, including studies reported earlier in the same article.

General discussion sections parallel discussions of single studies, except on a somewhat grander scale. They present all of the information contained in discussions of single studies, but consider the implications of all the studies presented together. A general discussion section brings the main ideas of a research program into bold relief. It typically begins with a concise summary of a research program's main findings, their relation to the original hypotheses, and their practical and theoretical implications. Thus, the summaries that begin general discussion sections are counterparts of the summaries that begin discussion sections of single study reports. Each presents a digest of the research presented in an article that can serve as both an organizing framework (when read first), and as a check on how well you have understood the main points of an article (when read last).

Research Reporting as Story Telling

A research report tells the story of how a researcher or group of researchers investigated a specific problem. Thus, a research report has a linear, narrative structure with a beginning, middle, and end. In his paper on writing research reports, Bem noted that a research report:

> ... is shaped like an hourglass. It begins with broad general statements, progressively narrows down to the specifics of [the] study, and then broadens out again to more general considerations. (1987, p. 175)

This format roughly mirrors the process of scientific investigation, wherein researchers do the following: (I) start with a broad idea from which they formulate a narrower set of hypotheses, informed by past empirical findings (introduction); (2) design a specific set of concrete operations to test these hypotheses (method); (3) analyze the observations collected in this way, and decide if they support the original hypotheses (results); and (4) explore the broader theoretical and practical implications of the findings, and consider how they contribute to an understanding of the problem under investigation (discussion). Though these stages are somewhat arbitrary distinctions—research actually proceeds in a number of different ways—they help elucidate the inner logic of research reports.

While reading a research report, keep this linear structure in mind. Though it is difficult to remember a series of seemingly disjointed facts, when these facts are joined together in a logical, narrative structure, they become easier to comprehend and recall. Thus, always remember that a research report tells a story. It will help you to organize the information you read, and remember it later.

Describing research reports as stories is not just a convenient metaphor. Research reports are stories. Stories can be said to consist of two components: A telling of what happened, and an explanation of why it happened. It is tempting to view science as an endeavor that simply catalogues facts, but nothing is further from the truth. The goal of science, social psychology included, is to explain facts, to explain why what happened happened. Social psychology is built on the dynamic interplay of discovery and justification, the dialogue between systematic observation of relations and their theoretical explanation. Though research reports do present novel facts based on systematic observation, these facts are presented in the service of ideas. Facts in isolation are trivia. Facts tied together by an explanatory theory are science. Therein lies the story. To really understand what researchers have to say, you need consider how their explanations relate to their findings.

The Rest of the Story

There is really no such thing as research.
There is only search, more search, keep
on searching.
(Bowering, 1988, p. 95)

Once you have read through a research report, and understand the researchers' findings and their explanations of them, the story does not end there. There is more than one interpretation for any set of findings. Different researchers often explain the same set of facts in different ways.

Let's take a moment to dispel a nasty rumor. The rumor is this: Researchers present their studies in a dispassionate manner, intending only to inform readers of their findings and their interpretation of those findings. In truth, researchers aim not only to inform readers, but also to persuade them (Sternberg, 1995). Researchers want to convince you their ideas are right. There is never only one explanation for a set of findings. Certainly, some explanations are better than others; some fit the available data better, are more parsimonious, or require fewer questionable assumptions. The point here is that researchers are very passionate about their ideas, and want you to believe them. It's up to you to decide if you want to buy their ideas or not.

Let's compare social psychologists to sales-clerks. Both social psychologists and salesclerks want to sell you something; either their ideas, or their wares. You need to decide if you want to buy what they're selling or not—and there are potentially negative consequences for either decision. If you let a sales clerk dazzle you with a sales pitch, without thinking about it carefully, you might end up buying a substandard product that you don't really need. After having done this a few times, people tend to become cynical, steeling themselves against any and all sales pitches. This too is dangerous. If you are overly critical of sales pitches, you could end up foregoing genuinely useful products. Thus, by analogy, when you are too critical in your reading of research reports,

you might dismiss, out of hand, some genuinely useful ideas—ideas that can help shed light on why people behave the way they do.

This discussion raises the important question of how critical one should be while reading a research report. In part, this will depend on why one is reading the report. If you are reading it simply to learn what the researchers have to say about a particular issue, for example, then there is usually no need to be overly critical. If you want to use the research as a basis for planning a new study, then you should be more critical. As you develop an understanding of psychological theory and research methods, you will also develop an ability to criticize research on many different levels. And any piece of research can be criticized at some level. As Jacob Cohen put it, "A successful piece of research doesn't conclusively settle an issue, it just makes some theoretical proposition to some degree more likely" (1990, p. 1311). Thus, as a consumer of research reports, you have to strike a delicate balance between being overly critical and overly accepting.

While reading a research report, at least initially, try to suspend your disbelief. Try to understand the researchers' story; that is, try to understand the facts-the findings and how they were obtained—and the suggested explanation of those facts-the researchers' interpretation of the findings and what they mean. Take the research to task only after you feel you understand what the authors are trying to say. Research reports serve not only an important archival function, documenting research and its findings, but also an invaluable stimulus function. They can excite other researchers to join the investigation of a particular issue, or to apply new methods or theory to a different, perhaps novel, issue. It is this stimulus function that Elliot Aronson, an eminent social psychologist, referred to when he admitted that, in publishing a study, he hopes his colleagues will "look at it, be stimulated by it, be provoked by it, annoyed by it, and then go ahead and do it better That's the exciting thing about science; it progresses by people taking off on one another's work" (1995, p. 5). Science is indeed a cumulative enterprise, and each new study builds on what has (or, sometimes, has not) gone before it. In this way, research articles keep social psychology vibrant.

A study can inspire new research in a number of different ways, such as: (1) it can lead one to conduct a better test of the hypotheses, trying to rule out alternative explanations of the findings; (2) it can lead one to explore the limits of the findings, to see how widely applicable they are, perhaps exploring situations to which they do not apply; (3) it can lead one to test the implications of the findings, furthering scientific investigation of the phenomenon; (4) it can inspire one to apply the findings, or a novel methodology, to a different area of investigation; and (5) it can provoke one to test the findings in the context of a specific real world problem, to see if they can shed light on it. All of these are excellent extensions of the original research, and there are, undoubtedly, other ways that research findings can spur new investigations.

The problem with being too critical, too soon, while reading research reports is that the only further research one may be willing to attempt is research of the first type: Redoing a study better. Sometimes this is desirable, particularly in the early stages of investigating a particular issue, when the findings are novel and perhaps unexpected. But redoing a reasonably compelling study, without extending it in any way, does little to advance our understanding of human behavior. Although the new study might be "better," it will not be "perfect," so it would have to be run again, and again, likely never reaching a stage where it is beyond criticism. At some point, researchers have to decide that the evidence is compelling enough to warrant investigation of the last four types. It is these types of studies that most advance our knowledge of social behavior. As you read more research reports, you will become more comfortable deciding when a study is "good enough" to move beyond it. This is a somewhat subjective judgment, and should be made carefully.

When social psychologists write up a research report for publication, it is because they believe they have something new and exciting to communicate about social behavior. Most research reports that are submitted for publication are rejected. Thus, the reports that are eventually published are deemed pertinent not only by the researchers who wrote them, but also by the reviewers and editors of the journals in which they are published. These people, at least, believe the research reports they write and publish have something important and interesting to say. Sometimes, you'll disagree; not all journal articles are created equal, after all. But we recommend that you, at least initially, give these well-meaning social psychologists the benefit of the doubt. Look for what they're excited about. Try to understand the authors' story, and see where it leads you.

References

American Psychological Association (1994). *Publication manual* (4th ed.). Washington, D.C.

Aronson, E. (1995). Research in social psychology as a leap of faith. In E. Aronson (Ed.), *Readings about the social animal* (7th ed., pp. 3–9). New York: W. H. Freeman and Company.

Bem, D. J. (1987). Writing the empirical journal article. In M. P. Zanna & J. M. Darley (Eds.), *The complete academic: A practical guide for the beginning social scientist* (pp. 171–201). New York: Random House.

Bowering, G. (1988). *Errata*. Red Deer, Alta.: Red Deer College Press.

Cohen, J. (1990). Things I have learned (so far). *American Psychologist, 45*, 1304–1312.

Forgas, J. P. (1994). Sad and guilty? Affective influences on the explanation of conflict in close relationships. *Journal of Personality and Social Psychology, 66*, 56–68.

Stemberg, R. J. (1995). *The psychologist's companion: A guide to scientific writing for students and researchers* (3rd ed.). Cambridge: Cambridge University Press.

Lab #3

Purpose:

- This lab is designed to teach you about APA publication formatting and writing.
- Get to know students on research project team.
- Become familiar with assigned research topic.

Objectives:

- Learn about APA style by discussing the Jordan & Zanna article and the following section entitled APA Formatting and Style Guide.
- Meet members of group for research project.

Homework:

- Read the article that your lab project will be based upon.
- Complete research article summary homework.

APA Formatting and Style Guide

Journal articles published in psychology and many other social sciences use a common format for structuring papers, citing sources, and reporting statistics: APA (American Psychological Association) Style. To some students, the strict rules of APA Style may seem arbitrary and unnecessary, but it is quite important for psychological scientists to use a common format when putting research papers together.

The common structure helps to ensure that all papers are thorough and easy to read. APA Style clarifies what information does and does not need to be cited, and informs us exactly how to document our sources. A consistent format for documenting sources guarantees accuracy and makes it clear to readers exactly where a given piece of information came from. This format also ensures that the authors of any cited research are appropriately credited and treated with respect.

In terms of reporting statistics, APA Style helps to ensure that any statistical information is presented at an appropriate level of detail and makes it clear to readers exactly what each number and symbol presented means. APA Style also dictates the format of tables and figures, with the goal of making them comprehensive and understandable.

Another way to think about the importance of APA Style is to imagine what it would be like if every psychologist cited their sources and presented their statistics in their own unique way.

All of those idiosyncrasies would become quite distracting and would take the emphasis away from the substance of the research. Non-standard statistical information would also make it virtually impossible for researchers to conduct *meta-analyses*, in which the results of several studies are combined to look for overall patterns and trends. To conduct a proper meta-analysis, certain pieces of statistical information are vital, and if they are not presented in a paper, the person conducting the meta-analysis would have to try and track down the necessary statistics by contacting the study authors, which can be time consuming and challenging (academics often move around, sometimes datasets are lost or misplaced, etc.).

On the following pages, we present an *APA Quick Style Guide for Citing Sources and Formatting Papers* that addresses students' most frequently asked questions about citations and general formatting issues. For additional questions on these topics, please consult the APA Publication Manual. Later in this book, we will talk about reporting statistics in APA Style.

APA Quick Style Guide for Citing Sources and Formatting Papers

Paper Structure

APA Style papers generally follow this format:

- Title page (Page 1)
  - Paper titles are usually 10–12 words in length.
- Abstract (Page 2)
  - Abstracts are usually 100–200 words and provide a concise summary of the research (exact length requirements vary across journals).
- Introduction (beginning on page 3)
  - The introduction is not explicitly labeled as such and simply begins after a restatement of the title on page 3.
- Methods
  - This section is usually divided into three subsections: Participants, Materials, and Procedure
- Results
- Discussion
- References
- Tables & figures

We will provide more information on the content of each these sections later in this book when you are assigned to write them as part of your own paper.

Headings

APA style papers are divided into standard sections (e.g., Methods, Results, Discussion); however, you will often want to break these down into subsections to make the paper easier to read (e.g., you might divide Results into subsections that address each hypothesis). Most undergraduate student projects are simple enough to require the use of only two or three levels of headings, but you may need more than that depending on your project. Standard APA Style heading structures are as follows:

Level 1 headings:
Centered, Boldface, Uppercase and Lowercase

Level 2 headings:
Left-aligned, Boldface, Uppercase and Lowercase

Level 3 headings:
Indented, boldface, lowercase followed by a period.

Level 4 headings:
Indented, boldface, italicized, lowercase followed by a period.

Level 5 headings:
Indented, italicized, lowercase followed by a period.

As a general rule of thumb, Methods, Results, and Discussion should always be treated as Level 1 headings. Within the Methods section, Participants, Materials, and Procedure should be treated as Level 2 headings.

In-Text Citations

When citing a source within the text of the paper, the most common format is to include the authors' surnames and year of publication in parentheses at the end of the sentence. For example:

Women are more likely than men to hope that their current "friend with benefits" turns into a romantic partner (Lehmiller, VanderDrift, & Kelly, 2011).

An alternative way of citing the same source would be to include the authors' surnames as part of the narrative. This format is not preferred because it focuses the reader on the author instead of the finding, but it is still technically acceptable. For example:

Lehmiller, VanderDrift, and Kelly (2011) found that women were more likely than men to hope that their current "friend with benefits" turns into a romantic partner.

The very first time you cite a source in text, you should list all of the authors' surnames. On the second and any subsequent citations, only the first author's surname should appear followed by "et al." For example, if the above source were cited a second time, it might appear as:

Both men and women reported that their primary reason for starting a "friends with benefits" relationship was sex (Lehmiller et al., 2011).

The one exception to the "et al." rule is that if a paper has six or more authors, it should *always* be cited as the first author's surname followed by "et al."

In-Text Quotations

Direct quotations from research papers should be used sparingly. Whenever possible, you should paraphrase (i.e., put into your own words) the findings of past studies. However, if you feel that a direct quote is important, it can be cited as such:

"Gender differences related to sex, though sometimes quite pronounced, are rarely as stable or immutable as they seem at first glance" (Conley, Moors, Matsick, Ziegler, & Valentine, 2011, p. 211).

References

At the end of your paper, all sources (e.g., journal articles, book chapters, websites) that you cited or quoted in text should appear so that readers know exactly what you were citing and how they can find it on their own. There are a multitude of APA citation formats depending upon the nature of your source and the number of authors, so we will provide just a few common examples here. For citation questions that are not explicitly addressed below, please consult the APA Publication Manual.

Typical journal article citations:

Conley, T. D., Moors, A. C., Matsick, J. L., Ziegler, A., & Valentine, B. A. (2011). Women, men, and the bedroom: Methodological and conceptual insights that narrow, reframe, and eliminate gender differences in sexuality. *Current Directions in Psychological Science, 20,* 296–300. doi: 10.1177/0963721411418467

Sears, D. O., & Henry, P. J. (2003). The origins of symbolic racism. *Journal of Personality and Social Psychology, 85,* 259–275. doi: 10.1037/0022-3514.85.2.259

Typical book citation:

Thibaut, J. W., & Kelley, H. H. (1959). *The social psychology of groups.* New York: Wiley.

Typical book chapter citation:

Graziano, W. G. & Bruce, J. W. (2008). Attraction and the initiation of relationships: A review of the empirical literature. In S. Sprecher, A. Wenzel & J. Harvey (Eds.), *Handbook of relationship initiation.* (pp. 269–296). New York: Psychology Press.

Typical website citation:

Wang, W. (2012). *The rise of intermarriage: Rates, characteristics vary by race and gender.* Retrieved from: http://www.pewsocialtrends.org/2012/02/16/the-rise-of-intermarriage/?src=prc-headline

Here are a couple of additional helpful pointers when it comes to creating your References page:

- Be sure to double check your punctuation, capitalization and italicizing before submitting your paper.
- List all authors' surnames and initials unless there are eight or more. In this case, list out only the first six authors followed by a series of three ellipses (i.e., …) and then the last author.
- Issue numbers are not required in parentheses after volume numbers unless the journal is paginated by issue (i.e., issue numbers are only required if the page numbers start back at 1 in each issue of the journal). Most journals are not paginated by issue, so issue numbers are not usually required.
- Be sure to include DOI numbers for journals if they exist.
- If you use a citation tool for generating your references in APA style (e.g., Endnote, Google Scholar), be sure to double check the format because they are often incorrect! In our experience, computer programs sometimes generate more errors than students do on their own, so be wary of taking shortcuts.

Research Article Summary Homework

After reading the original article that your research project will be based on this semester, you will turn in a short summary of the article for the next lab meeting. Your summary should be in the following format:

I. Background of the study:
   Give a reference citation (be sure to use APA format *exactly*).
   Goal/Purpose of the study.
II. Method:
   Participants (be specific).
   Materials/Measures used.
   Procedure.

III. Results:
   State what they found (don't report actual statistics).
IV. Study Importance:
   State why this study is important, and what new information it provided to the field of social psychology.

Your summary should be about one page long, double spaced, using 12-point font. Print one copy for your instructor and one for yourself, and bring them to the next lab.

LITERATURE REVIEWS

Lab #4

Purpose:

- The purpose of this lab is to learn how to conduct a literature search using PsycINFO.

Objectives:

- Discuss research article with group members.
- Develop search terms for literature search.
- Learn how to use PsycINFO on lab computers.
- Identify background articles for study.

Homework:

- Search for (using PsycINFO) and obtain two research articles that are related to your study. Write up draft summaries of them to present to your lab group during lab #5. You will submit final versions of these summaries to the instructor for grading during lab #6.
- Start *thinking* about some related hypotheses you are interested in testing out for your project.

Using PsycINFO

PsycINFO is an electronic database of articles, book chapters, edited books, dissertation abstracts, etc., related to the field of psychology. You will have to use PsycINFO this week to locate two articles that are related to your research topic. Your instructor will show you in class how to access PsycINFO through the library.

For your homework: If the library has an electronic copy of the article, you may be able to download it directly. If not, you will not have time to order it via interlibrary loan. If the library owns the journal, you will need to go there to copy it directly from the bound journal. The library likely owns most of the journals you will be locating. If the library does not have a link for an electronic copy or hard copies in their facility, locate another article for now. You can also order the article for later use when writing your final paper.

Note: **E-mail your research team members to be sure that you are not locating the same articles.** If you use different search terms, this should not be a problem. But before beginning to write your assignment, be sure you all have two different articles.

Useful websites:
http://www.muhlenberg.edu/depts/psychology/FindReadCite.htm
http://www.apa.org/pubs/databases/training/ebsco.pdf

Literature Review

Review of Relevant Literature

BEFORE even beginning to develop a research idea, you need to conduct a literature review to see what has been done before, and what questions remain to be answered. To successfully write the Introduction and Discussion sections of an APA-formatted report for this class, you must have a basic understanding of the purpose of the studies reviewed, their subject populations tested, the methods used, and the results and conclusions of prior studies.

Reviewing an Introduction Section

The Introduction section should provide you with the rationale and purpose of the study. A useful strategy to understand the studies reviewed in the Introduction is to read the first and last paragraphs before reading the remaining paragraphs. The first paragraph should provide you with a general description of the problem to be studied, and the final paragraph should provide you with a specific idea/purpose to be tested in the experiment. All paragraphs in between are usually designed to illustrate why the specific question (hypothesis) tested in the experiment is useful to gain information about the general problem described in the first paragraph.

Reviewing a Method Section

The Method section will provide you with information about participants, apparatus, and procedure.

Participants: This experiment tested _____ groups with _____ participants in each group.

Apparatus and procedure: Find and define for yourself the independent or predictor variable(s) and the dependent variable(s). The procedure in an experiment will always involve definition of the task the subjects are asked to perform (dependent variable) in each testing group/condition (independent variable).

Reviewing a Results Section

The Results section will present graphs and/or tables and text that describe the changes in the participants' behavior (dependent variable) that occurred in response to changes in the experimental variable (independent variable). Or—how do people's actions differ, based on which category they are in?

Reviewing a Discussion Section

The Discussion section should provide you with a "what it all means" summary. This section is the grand finale to ideas presented in the Introduction section, because the Discussion will attempt to: 1) show how findings of this experiment add to past knowledge; and 2) indicate questions still unanswered and hypotheses that need to be tested in the future. At this point, it would be useful to review the information you extracted from the Introduction section, because these issues will be addressed again in the Discussion section.

Summary of Reviewing Relevant Literature

You have now extracted enough information to use this article as a reference for your study. You will most likely use this information in your paper's Introduction section to relate information provided in this study to the purposes of your own study. You will also compare the findings of this study with your own study's findings in the Discussion section.

Homework Assignment: PsycINFO Search

For this assignment, you will conduct a small literature search on your research topic in order to locate materials that will help you in generating hypotheses, and aid in the writing of your research paper.

1. Generate a number of search terms to use. These can be keywords from your primary article, the author's name, a research topic or method contained within the article, etc.
2. Go onto the PsycINFO search engine through the library website, and use your search terms to generate a list of articles, chapters, etc.
3. Read through titles and abstracts that look most interesting to you. Select two different **research articles**. This means that they are articles where one or several studies were conducted, *not a meta-analysis, review, or theoretical paper.* If you see any other articles that are interesting, you can get them and use them later for your Introduction/ literature review in your final paper, but for this assignment, you only need 2 *separate* research articles. If an article reports more than one study, this still only counts as one article, and you will need to provide a summary of the whole article (all studies). You will need two total articles for this assignment.
4. Be sure that your new articles are different from those of your research team members. *If there are any duplicates, you will not receive credit for that particular summary.*
5. Get the articles from the library and read them.

6. Next, you will prepare a summary of the new articles that you will turn in to your lab group members (during lab #5) and instructor (during lab #6). Each summary should be in the following format:

I. Background of the study:
Give a reference citation (be sure to use APA format *exactly*).
Goal/Purpose of the study.
II. Method:
Participants (be specific).
Materials/Measures used.
Procedure.
III. Results:
State what they found (do not report actual statistics).
IV. Study Relevance:
State how this study is important and related to your research topic.

You will write <u>one summary for each article.</u> Each summary should be at least one page long, double spaced, using 12-point font. Print a copy for each member of your research team (including yourself) for lab #5. You will submit final copies of these summaries to the instructor during lab #6, after you've had a chance to revise them, based on feedback from your first article summary assignment (which will be handed back in lab #5).

NON-EXPERIMENTAL
RESEARCH DESIGNS

Lab #5

Purpose:

- This lab is an introduction to nonexperimental research designs.

Objectives:

- Go over results of research teams' literature searches.
- Review the following section entitled Non-Experimental Research Designs and discuss when and how these methods are utilized in social psychological research.

Homework:

- Use the feedback from your first article summary assignment to revise the two draft article summaries you brought in today. You will submit final versions of these two article summaries to the instructor at the next lab.

Non-Experimental Research Designs

NON-EXPERIMENTAL research designs do not involve the manipulation of any variables. These designs are an essential research tool for social psychologists because we cannot always manipulate the variables that are of interest to us. For example, we cannot randomly assign people to a gender, a relationship type, or a political affiliation. There are several types of non-experimental designs, including descriptive, correlational, ex-post facto, and longitudinal. **Descriptive studies** involve simply observing and describing a phenomenon or the frequency/occurrence of a behavior. **Correlational designs** consider the statistical relationship that one variable has with another. **Ex-post facto designs** involve comparing two or more groups on a variable of interest, but those groups differ in some important way (e.g., gender, race, nationality). One other type of non-experimental design is a **longitudinal study**, in which you measure responses over a period of time and do not directly manipulate any variables. In all of these cases, the researcher is either examining behaviors or outcomes as they naturally occur, outcomes that have already occurred, or how specific variables are associated with each other (note that "associated" does NOT mean that the one variable caused changes in another).

Non-experimental designs are conducted in much the same way as experimental designs. You begin by developing your research question and hypothesis, and then identifying the variables of interest. However, you cannot manipulate an independent variable in non-experimental research (independent variables are defined here as those variables that cannot be, should not be, or were not manipulated, such as gender, relationship type, political affiliation, etc.). As a result, non-experimental researchers often assess **control variables** in their studies, which are variables that you think could potentially serve as alternative explanations for your observed findings. For example, if you were interested in the association between ethnic group membership and attitudes towards one's primary care physician, you might also want to measure how long each participant has been in the United States and their general feelings about Western medicine, because these variables could potentially explain any differences you ultimately find in physician attitudes across groups. In other words, if one ethnic group exhibited more positive attitudes toward their doctors than another ethnic group, you would not just want to assume that the results were entirely due to differences in participants' ethnicity. However, you can build somewhat more confidence in that conclusion if you can show that the groups do not differ in other ways (e.g., attitudes toward Western medicine), or if the findings still hold even when you statistically correct for your control variables (e.g., by including them as predictor variables in a regression model).

When you interpret non-experimental research results, it is important to avoid committing the **post-hoc fallacy**, which refers to the tendency to assume that when we observe two variables occur closely in time that one necessarily caused the other. For example, imagine that you conducted an observational study of kids on a playground and noticed that a young boy responded with aggression after being provoked, but a young girl did not become aggressive after similar provocation. You might be tempted to conclude that provocation causes aggression in boys but not in girls. However, no variables were directly manipulated in this case, so it is not safe to draw any conclusions about cause and effect. Other factors could have been present in your study (e.g., individual differences in personality between the boy and the girl), and without direct manipulation and strict controls, it is hard to rule out other such possibilities that could potentially explain your findings.

EXPERIMENTAL AND QUASI-EXPERIMENTAL DESIGN

Lab #6

Purpose:

- This lab is designed to teach you about experimental and quasi-experimental designs.

Objectives:

- Review the following section entitled Experimental and Quasi-Experimental Research and discuss when and how these methods are utilized in social psychological research.
- Complete in-class research design activity. Your instructor will assign you to complete one of the four activities that appear on the following pages.

Homework:

- Study for quiz on labs #2–6.

Experimental and Quasi-Experimental Research

THE goal of experimental research is to examine the effect of one variable on another variable. Specifically, scientists manipulate the **independent variable** (e.g., level of alcohol consumption) in order to see what effect this has on the **dependent variable** (e.g., decision-making ability). The appeal of experiments is that they are the only research design that allows us to make inferences about cause and effect. To the extent that changes in the independent variable are accompanied by changes in the dependent variable, we can infer that one likely caused the other.

Our ability to infer causation fundamentally depends upon whether **random assignment** to experimental conditions was present. When random assignment is present, we have a true experiment; when random assignment is not present, we have what is known as a quasi-experiment.

True Experiments

In a true experiment, each participant must have an equal chance of being assigned to each level or condition of the independent variable. To illustrate this, let us say we are conducting a study on how exposure to gendered media portrayals (the independent variable) affects endorsement of traditional gender role beliefs (the dependent variable). Let us further say that our independent variable has two levels: a 10-minute video portraying men and women in very stereotypical terms, and a 10-minute video portraying men and women in counter-stereotypical terms. If we randomly assign participants to conditions (e.g., by flipping a coin or using a computer program to decide which video each person will watch), participants will have an equal chance of being assigned to watch each video. The result of this is that the group of participants who see the stereotypic video should be very similar to the group of participants who see the counter-stereotypic video. To the extent that the groups are similar, it helps rule out the possibility that something other than the independent variable (i.e., a **confounding variable**) might be responsible for any observed changes in the dependent variable.

In addition to random assignment, researchers can further reduce the risk of confounding variables entering the picture by tightly controlling all aspects of the experiment. This means making sure that the independent variable is the only one thing that is changing in each condition. In our example study about gendered media portrayals, this means that we would want to make sure that all participants watched their assigned video in the same room where things like temperature and lighting could be held constant, distractions could be kept to a minimum, and all participants could interact with the same research assistant. The more things that vary across conditions, the more "noise" you introduce and the harder it becomes to pinpoint the causal factor(s).

Of course, all of this control comes at the cost of producing artificial conditions that may not accurately represent what happens in the real world. This is the classic trade-off between internal and external validity. The more that you maximize **internal validity** by trying to ensure that nothing other than the independent variable is being manipulated, the more you sacrifice external validity (i.e., your ability to generalize the findings beyond the lab setting).

True experiments can take many forms depending upon how many independent variables you want to examine, how you plan to manipulate your variables, and what type of comparison level you want to use to determine the effectiveness of your experimental manipulation. With regard to number of variables, **one-way experiments** include a single independent variable; **factorial experiments** include two or more. The advantage of factorial experiments is that they provide the ability to test for statistical **interactions** (i.e., does the effect of one independent variable differ at levels of another independent variable?). With regard to how variables are manipulated, an independent variable can be manipulated **between subjects** (known as a nested design) or **within subjects** (known as a crossed design). In a between subjects design, each participant receives only one level of the independent variable, whereas in a within subjects design, each participant receives all levels of the independent variable at some point. Each design has its own unique advantages and disadvantages (e.g., within subjects designs require fewer participants, but there is the potential that giving the same person multiple manipulations may produce interference across conditions). Finally, with regard to the comparison level, one option would be to take a baseline measurement at the beginning of the study and compare that to a post-manipulation assessment. Alternatively, you could include a control condition in your study to see what happens to participants when the independent variable is absent.

Quasi-Experiments

Sometimes a true experiment is not possible to conduct because it is unethical or infeasible to employ random assignment. In such cases, a scientist may conduct a quasi-experiment instead (i.e., a study that resembles an experiment in many ways, but that lacks random assignment). An **ex-post facto** study, previously discussed, would be considered one type of quasi-experiment. Let us consider an example: if an applied social psychologist wanted to study the effect of seatbelt laws on automobile injuries and fatalities, a true experiment would not be possible because psychologists do not have the power to change the law (and even if they did, it would be unethical to do so just to see what happens). Instead, a researcher might compare two U.S. states where seatbelt laws differ, such as New Hampshire (where seatbelts are not required) and Maine (where seatbelts are required). The researcher might then compare how many injuries and fatalities were reported in each state during the last two years.

Quasi-experiments may be **retrospective**, meaning they identify groups now and look back in time, or they may be **prospective**, meaning they identify groups now and follow them into the future. Either way, due to the lack of random assignment, quasi-experiments suffer from the same limitation, known as the **third variable problem**. This refers to the fact that some third variable the researchers have not accounted for may be responsible for any observed effects rather than the independent variable. It could be that the groups you are comparing are different in some way (e.g., in our example study about seatbelt laws, perhaps the speed limits also differ between states. Perhaps the types of cars on the road differ as well). There is also the possibility that historical and other unplanned events can affect the dependent variable, given how little control the researcher has in a study of this nature.

Thus, our ability to infer cause and effect is much more limited in a quasi-experiment than it is in a true experiment; however, quasi-experiments are sometimes the best and only option for addressing certain research questions.

Lab Group Exercise: Group 1

Research Topic: The relationship between self-esteem and test performance.

1. Design a correlational study to investigate the relationship between these two variables. What is your hypothesis? How will you operationally define and measure the two variables?

2. How will you obtain a random sample of participants?

3. Assume that your study produces a correlation of .56 between the two variables. What are at least three possible causal explanations for this relationship?

4. Now design an experimental study to investigate these variables. What is your hypothesis? What type of hypothesis does the experimental method allow you to test that the correlational method does not?

5. What is your independent variable? What is your dependent variable?

6. How will you use random assignment to conditions?

7. Do any ethical concerns about the treatment of participants emerge from your experimental design?

Lab Group Exercise: Group 2

Research Topic: The relationship between the amount of time couples spend together and their relationship satisfaction.

1. Design a correlational study to investigate the relationship between these two variables. What is your hypothesis? How will you operationally define and measure the two variables?

2. How will you obtain a random sample of participants?

3. Assume that your study produces a correlation of .56 between the two variables. What are at least three possible causal explanations for this relationship?

4. Now design an experimental study to investigate these variables. What is your hypothesis? What type of hypothesis does the experimental method allow you to test that the correlational method does not?

5. What is your independent variable? What is your dependent variable?

6. How will you use random assignment to conditions?

7. Do any ethical concerns about the treatment of participants emerge from your experimental design?

Lab Group Exercise: Group 3

Research Topic: The relationship between listening to heavy metal music and aggression.

1. Design a correlational study to investigate the relationship between these two variables. What is your hypothesis? How will you operationally define and measure the two variables?

2. How will you obtain a random sample of participants?

3. Assume that your study produces a correlation of .56 between the two variables. What are at least three possible causal explanations for this relationship?

4. Now design an experimental study to investigate these variables. What is your hypothesis? What type of hypothesis does the experimental method allow you to test that the correlational method does not?

5. What is your independent variable? What is your dependent variable?

6. How will you use random assignment to conditions?

7. Do any ethical concerns about the treatment of participants emerge from your experimental design?

Lab Group Exercise: Group 4

Research Topic: The relationship between the physical attractiveness of a political candidate and voters' opinion of him or her.

1. Design a correlational study to investigate the relationship between these two variables. What is your hypothesis? How will you operationally define and measure the two variables?

2. How will you obtain a random sample of participants?

3. Assume that your study produces a correlation of .56 between the two variables. What are at least three possible causal explanations for this relationship?

4. Now design an experimental study to investigate these variables. What is your hypothesis? What type of hypothesis does the experimental method allow you to test that the correlational method does not?

5. What is your independent variable? What is your dependent variable?

6. How will you use random assignment to conditions?

7. Do any ethical concerns about the treatment of participants emerge from your experimental design?

HYPOTHESIS
DEVELOPMENT

Lab #7

Purpose:

- Learn about the development of hypotheses and operationalization.

Objectives:

- Take a quiz on labs #2–6.
- Review the following section entitled Research Questions, as well as the section entitled Hypothesis Development and Operationalization. Discuss best practices for developing research questions and hypotheses.

Homework:

- Complete hypothesis development assignment.

Research Questions

THE first step toward developing a hypothesis is to have a good research question. Research questions are clear and focused questions upon which you base your research—they set the goals for what you want to study. The question moves you from what is known, to what requires further validation because it is unknown. You develop your research question by taking the following steps:

1. Select a topic that you are interested in pursuing. By selecting or being assigned a springboard article for this class, you will have a topic that you are already curious about, or at least invested in researching.
2. Get a good understanding of the topic. You will survey the literature to get a sense of the research that has already been conducted on your topic in order to get a good understanding of what research questions have already been asked, and what was found. This initial survey of the literature can help you refine what additional research questions remain to be answered. As you read, jot down questions in the margins of the articles. What do you know from your other classes or from your personal experiences that you can apply or extend the research to?
3. Start asking some open-ended questions about why certain results were found. Also, how did the process described take place? Generate as many open ended questions as you can based on your topic and springboard article.
4. Select the questions that you find most interesting and evaluate them. Are the questions complex enough to examine for your project? The question should not be answerable with a simple "yes" or "no." The question should require more literature searching and research in order to better answer it. Is your question focused enough? Your question needs to be complex, but also focused in order to make it feasible for your project for this class. Is your question clear enough? There is so much published research out there already that an unclear question can make narrowing down your literature search more difficult.
5. Hypothesize. After you have your research question, then you can rewrite your question into a testable form, the hypothesis, which then leads to the identification of the variables for your study.

Examples of research questions

Unclear: *Why are social networking sites like Facebook bad for relationships?*
Clear: *How does sharing relationship information on Facebook impact ratings of relationship satisfaction for partners?*

The unclear statement is not specific in terms of what "bad" means or what behaviors on Facebook are of concern. There should not be ambiguity in the research question.

Unfocused: *What is the effect of prejudice on quality of life?*

Focused: *What is the impact of workplace discrimination on self-esteem?*

The unfocused question is so broad that even a book could not address it in its entirety. The focused question specified what type of outcome was of interest (self-esteem), and a specific form of discrimination that could have an impact on it.

Too simple: *How many friendships do people lose after they graduate from college?*

Appropriately complex: *What interpersonal factors contribute to friendship termination after college graduation?*

The simple question is something that can be easily looked up on-line or located in a survey and answered with a few factual sentences. There is no room for interpretation or analysis. The more complex version is a thought provoking question that requires you to dig deeper and investigate. If you can Bing or Google your research question and get an answer, your question is probably too simple.

Hypothesis Development and Operationalization

AFTER you have decided upon a research question, you will need to convert it into a testable hypothesis. There are many definitions for the term "hypothesis," but we suggest that you think of hypotheses as testable predictions about what you think will happen in a given study. Hypotheses are often phrased as "if- then" statements, such as "if _____ occurs, then _____ will (or will not) occur." Hypotheses are not moral or ethical questions; rather, they are just predictions about how specific variables are related to each other.

There are three qualities that a good hypothesis should possess:

1. It is testable, meaning that you can obtain evidence demonstrating whether the statement is likely correct or incorrect.
2. It is falsifiable, meaning that you should be able to acquire results that could potentially show that your hypothesis is *not* true.
3. It is succinct, meaning that it should be phrased simply and to the point.

A good hypothesis is also specific. For example, it would not be a good idea to hypothesize the following because it is too vague: "our ability to control portion size at meal time is *correlated* with our body mass index (BMI)." You need to clarify what specific type of correlation you expect. Is ability to control portion size negatively or positively associated with BMI?

There are actually two hypotheses that are tested in any given study: 1) the **null hypothesis**, which specifies that there is no relationship between the variables being studied, and 2) the **alternative hypothesis**, which specifies that a relationship exists between the variable. If you write out the null and alternative hypotheses, they should therefore be polar opposites. At the end of your statistical analyses, you will either **reject** or **fail to reject** the null hypothesis. If you reject the null hypothesis, then you tentatively accept that the alternative hypothesis it true (i.e., an association exists). If you fail to reject the null, you do not necessarily accept that that null is true—rather, you simply conclude that there is not enough evidence available to reject it, at least not yet. Although this language (i.e., reject vs. fail to reject) may sound awkward, it is preferred by statisticians because it is precise. Please keep in mind that although most published studies in social psychology are technically based upon null hypothesis testing, you will usually only see the alternative hypothesis written out and discussed in most of these journal articles.

After you have written your hypotheses, you will need to operationalize your variables. This means that you need to identify exactly how you will manipulate and measure each of the variables in your study. For example, if your hypothesis is that individuals with high self-esteem will be less likely to aggress against out-group members when threated, you need to now indicate how you will measure self-esteem and aggression, as well as how you will manipulate the terms "out-group" and "threat." Of course, keep in mind that each researcher may have their own ideas about what constitutes a valid operationalization of each variable. For example, one researcher may believe the decibels of a noise blast administered to persons in another room can reveal a person's aggressive tendencies, whereas others may not buy this operationalization. Therefore, as you decide how you will operationalize your variables, you must consider what is standard or "acceptable" practice by other researchers in the field, and be able to justify the your own operationalization (especially if you do something that has never been done before). For instance, if you decide you want to write your own survey questions to assess self-esteem, chances are you will need to provide a *very* good justification for not using one of the standardized measures of self-esteem that have been used extensively for decades.

Hypothesis Development Homework

AFTER reading about the study upon which your research project is based, as well as the literature that you and your research team have collected, your homework is to now think about how you might change the study. You are going to generate **two** hypotheses, and think of some methods to examine them. You will turn in one copy to the instructor, and the other you will discuss within your research group. Be prepared to present the logic for your responses.

One thing to bear in mind as you do this assignment: Base your hypotheses on the literature review you and your team just conducted. When you think about an idea you want to test out, think about WHY you want to test it. What literature support makes you think that your hypothesis is worth testing? If you want to test group differences (male versus female, old versus young, etc.), *why* would you expect those differences, based on what you read? What theoretical or empirical rationale can you give for why you want to test what you do? *Be careful here.* If you start pulling theories/studies that are not in your current literature search, you will have to conduct another one for your final paper!

For your assignment next week, answer the following questions:

1. What additional (*different*) hypotheses can you generate that **would be related to** the original study? (It might help to think about whether there are other explanations for the results: if results would be different in another sample, etc.). You can bring in information from the other studies you found in your literature review, as well as the original study itself. Think carefully about *why* you believe your hypothesis is worth testing. Write out **two** hypotheses (not to exceed two sentences each).

2. Discuss WHY your hypotheses are worth testing. What empirical or theoretical support can you provide (based on your literature searches) that would make you predict what you do? (Not to exceed three sentences each.)

3. Briefly and generally, describe the method of your study (how would *you* go about collecting data necessary for your hypothesis testing) for *each* hypothesis. This should not exceed one or two paragraphs for each one. If the method would be the same for both hypotheses, be sure to explain why.

The length of this paper will vary, depending on how much detail and work you put into your ideas. Papers *usually* range from two to three pages. Type this paper up using 12-point font, double spaced. Be sure to check for grammatical errors and use spell check! **Print two copies**, one for your instructor, and one to reference in your lab group discussion during the next class.

Below is an example of the type of information that might be provided for this assignment.

What might a sample hypothesis look like?*

Topic: Close relationships and emotions

Individuals perceiving that their relationship needs are met by their partner will experience more positive emotions and fewer negative emotions than individuals whose needs remain unfulfilled.

What might a rationale for the hypothesis look like?

Based on interdependence theory, and the literature on goals and emotions, having one's needs fulfilled in his or her relationship is akin to attaining one's relationship goals. Therefore, it is likely that positive emotions will follow from need fulfillment; negative emotions are produced by a lack of need fulfillment in a relationship.

What might a description of the methods look like?

First, it would be necessary to define and identify "relationship needs," and construct a way to measure those needs. Most likely, these will be related to having a partner to talk to, do stuff with, and be intimate with. A pilot study will probably be necessary to identify these needs,

or maybe there is existing literature on relationship needs that we can draw from. Participants will be (approximately 100) college students who are currently involved in romantic relationships. They will be asked to rate statements related to the extent to which their partners fulfill their needs (for example, "today my partner met my needs for closeness") each day (i.e., like a daily-diary study). In addition, they will report the extent to which they experienced certain emotions each day as well (today I felt: happy, angry, depressed, etc.). It is predicted that those whose needs were met on each day will report more positive emotions than those whose needs were not met (i.e., a positive correlation between need fulfillment and positive emotions); those whose needs were not met are expected to report more negative emotions than those whose needs were met (i.e., a negative correlation between need fulfillment and negative emotion).

It might also be interesting to make this a "couples" study, in which both members of the relationship participate. Then, one could investigate the extent to which one partner's report of needs provided (i.e., "I provided emotional support") corresponds with the other partner's report of needs fulfilled (i.e., "I received emotional support"), and if one partner's provided needs predicts the other partner's emotional experience.

---

* Hypothesis developed by Benjamin Le, Ph.D., Haverford University: http://www.haveerford.edu/psych/ble/teaching/psy325/hyp.htm

MEASUREMENT

Lab #8

Purpose:

- The purpose of the lab this week is to learn more about measurement issues in research.
- Rank order possible hypotheses for project.

Objectives:

- Discuss the following section entitled Measurement. Learn about different measurement scales as well as important measurement considerations.
- Research teams meet to discuss their hypotheses with each other, and narrow down the top three hypotheses they are interested in investigating.

Homework:

- None!

Measurement

MEASUREMENT refers to the act of assigning values to each level of a variable. No matter what type of study you might be conducting, measurement is an issue you must carefully consider. There are four main types of measurement scales that social psychologists utilize: nominal, ordinal, interval, and ratio. The specific scale you use will affect the types of statistical analyses you can conduct and the conclusions that can be drawn.

Nominal scales are the simplest form of measurement and involve assigning symbols or words to certain categories. As such, nominal scales are technically considered to be qualitative (or categorical) instead of quantitative because the data are classified according to types instead of amounts. Examples of variables that would be measured on nominal scales include gender, race, and personality (e.g., Type A vs. Type B). Sometimes, numbers are assigned to nominal variables to make them easier to work with in statistical analyses (e.g., you might code gender as 1 for female, 2 for male, and 3 for transgendered); however, these numbers are nothing more than markers to designate groups.

Ordinal scales are a form of measurement that provides information about rank; however, the intervals between each point on the scale are not equal and may be unknown. Thus, although ordinal scales may allow you to say that one person scored higher than another, they do not allow you to say how much higher that person scored. An example of an ordinal scale would be ranking students in order based upon their exam performance. Such a scale would allow you to conclude that the student ranked first had the highest score; however, we would not know whether first place just barely edged out second place, or if there was a dramatic difference between them.

Interval scales are similar to ordinal scales, except that the intervals between points on the scale are equal. These scales therefore allow you to determine not only how a set of values are ordered, but also how much difference there is between each value. An example of an interval scale would be IQ scores. The difference between a score of 100 and 101 is the same as the difference between a score of 125 and 126.

Ratio scales are very similar to interval scales, with one exception: they have a *true zero* (i.e., a point on the scale where zero means none, or the absence of the quality being assessed). Examples of ratio scales include income and weight.

You can think of all four of these scales as building upon each other, with each higher-order scale having all of the properties of the preceding scale(s). Thus, ratio scales have all of the properties of nominal, ordinal, and interval scales. It is also important to think about what type of analysis you plan on conducting, because this will inform how you should measure your outcome variable(s). For example, if your outcome variable is nominal, you will not be able to use ANOVA or linear regression; rather, you will need non-parametric statistics, such as Chi-Square.

Selecting the appropriate measurement scale for your analysis is just the beginning when it comes to measurement concerns. Social psychologists also need to ensure that the way they have chosen to measure their variables is both valid and reliable. In other words, we need to be confident that we are measuring what we think we are measuring (**validity**), and we need to be sure that our measurement tool has an acceptable level of consistency (**reliability**). In the absence of established validity and reliability, it is difficult to have any confidence in the findings of a given study.

Validity and reliability can be established in multiple ways. For example, to argue that a test is valid, we might consider **face validity** (does the test look like it is measuring what it is supposed to be measuring?), **content validity** (does the test capture the relevant dimensions of the construct?), **convergent validity** (does the test correlate positively with similar tests?), and/or **discriminant validity** (does the test correlate only mildly or not at all with dissimilar tests?). In addition, to argue that a test is reliable, we might check for **internal consistency reliability** (are all of the items within the scale highly correlated?) and/or **test-retest reliability** (are people's scores on the test consistent across time?). These are just a few of the many ways that social psychologists might demonstrate validity and reliability for their chosen measurement methods.

The key point to take away from this is that, whenever possible, it is best to select measurement tools for which researchers have already established validity and reliability. Of course, that is not always possible and, in such cases, it is wise to avoid creating a measurement scale in haste. It is important to think carefully about how you will measure each and every variable in your study to ensure that others' can be confident in your methods and results.

SURVEY PROCEDURES

Lab #9

Purpose:

- The purpose of this lab is to become more familiar with survey procedures.

Objectives:

- Review the following section entitled Survey Procedures and discuss when and how this method is utilized in social psychological research, as well as its unique advantages and disadvantages.
- Learn about different types of research questions that can be answered with this procedure.
- Discuss cross-sectional, repeated cross-sectional, panel, and experimental surveys.
- Discuss modes of survey administration (face-to-face and telephone interviews, self-administered, etc.).
- Learn basic issues surrounding questionnaire design and measurement error (response options, rating scale formats, order of alternatives, wording, etc.).
- Do in-class survey questionnaire wording exercise.
- Read and discuss two sample survey Method sections.

Homework:

- Read pages 342–348 of the Neighbors *et al.* (2002) article, and complete the survey validation worksheet.

Survey Procedures

Survey research involves collecting self-report data on people's attitudes, behaviors, and experiences via a carefully selected sample. Surveys can take many forms and can be administered in person, by telephone, or through mail or email. This flexible format allows researchers the ability to adapt surveys to meet their own needs, as well as the needs of their participants.

Surveys can be incorporated into research designs in many ways. Perhaps most commonly, psychologists utilize **cross-sectional surveys**, in which data are collected from one group of people at one point in time. The tradeoff with cross-sectional surveys is that while they are relatively easy to administer, they allow us to draw only very limited conclusions. A more powerful tool is the **panel survey** (also known as a longitudinal survey), in which data are collected from the same group of people at different points in time. Panel surveys are much more challenging to administer because of **attrition** (i.e., participants dropping out of the survey), but they are valuable for allowing us to see how attitudes and behaviors change across time. It is also worth noting that in both cross-sectional and panel surveys, experiments can be embedded within them if desired.

Regardless of which design and format is utilized, the success of a given survey depends upon the quality of the sample selected. Before conducting a survey, researchers must identify their **target population**, the group they are interested

in studying. Because it is impossible to study every single person in the target population, a **sample** or smaller group of people is selected to participate. Ideally, samples will be drawn through **random selection**. This occurs when everyone within the target population can be identified and a certain number of them are invited at random to take part in the study. When random selection is correctly implemented, each person in the target population has an equal chance of being selected, which results in a sample that is representative of the overall population. However, random selection is difficult, expensive, and time-consuming. As a result, **convenience sampling** occurs far more often, in which those individuals who are most accessible are asked to participate (e.g., college students). However, the obvious drawback to convenience sampling is that it limits our ability to make generalizations about the findings because the sample may not adequately reflect the broader population.

The other key to developing a successful survey is to take great care when developing and ordering the questions on your survey. To that end, researchers must carefully choose the language that appears in each question to make sure it is unambiguous and does not make unfair assumptions about participants. It is also important to avoid both **leading questions** and **double-barreled questions**. Leading questions are those that "lead" participants to a certain answer and discourage honest reporting (e.g., "Most college students think that marijuana should be legalized everywhere. Do you support legalizing marijuana?"). Double-barreled questions are those that ask participants two or more things at once, thereby resulting in a muddled answer (e.g., "Are you satisfied with the cost and quality of your college education?"). Researchers must also consider the order in which questions will appear on a survey, because early questions may affect how participants respond to later questions. For instance, if you wanted to ask participants how they feel about "equality for all Americans," their response to that question might be different if they were asked to complete a measure of racism beforehand because they will now be thinking about "equality" in racial terms.

In addition to thinking carefully about question wording and order, researchers must also consider the most appropriate response options to accompany each question. In some cases, an open-ended response may be desired (for qualitative studies), but other times closed questions with a preset list of response options are preferred (for quantitative studies). Closed questions may ask participants to rate their attitudes on a scale (e.g., ranging from "strongly disagree" to "strongly agree"), or they may ask participants to rank order a set of response options (e.g., participants might read about a problem and then rank their preferred solutions). The response option you choose has important implications for how you will be able to analyze and interpret your data (for more on this, consult the section on Measurement in this book).

Advantages and Disadvantages of Surveys

The main advantage of surveys is that they allow us to collect large amounts of data from many people in a short period of time. This is especially true for Internet-based surveys, which have the added benefit of increasing demographic diversity over samples drawn from college student subject pools (Gosling, Vazire, Srivastava, & John, 2004). Online surveys are also advantageous in offering enhanced anonymity for participants, which may increase honesty in responding. Also, as noted above, the flexible format and design of surveys makes them incredibly appealing compared to other research methods.

That said, surveys have some important limitations. For one thing, even when random selection is implemented, it is usually far from perfect due to the issue of **nonresponse**. In other words, not everyone who is contacted will be willing or available to participate in a given study. If the people who refuse to participate or who are unavailable are different from the rest of the population in some way (e.g., in terms of personality or demographics), the end result is an unrepresentative sample. The other side of this coin is known as **volunteer bias** or self-selection. This refers to the fact that people who volunteer to participate in research may be different from the rest of the population in some way (e.g., perhaps volunteers are more helpful in general), thereby producing an unrepresentative sample. As some evidence of volunteer bias, research has found that persons who agree to participate in studies of sexual behavior are more sexually experienced than those who choose not to participate in such studies (Plaud, Gaither, Hegstad, Rowan, & Devitt, 1999)

Another potential problem with surveys is the issue of **socially desirable responding**, which occurs when people intentionally try to present themselves in the most favorable manner possible. This may take the form of skipping certain questions or giving an answer that makes one look good, even though it is not the truth. Providing participants with complete anonymity and guaranteeing confidentiality of their results helps to reduce this tendency, but it does not get rid of it completely because some people may not wish to admit or reveal certain things about themselves under any circumstances (e.g., experiences with infidelity).

References

Gosling, S.D., Vazire, S., Srivastava, S., & John, O.P. (2004). Should we trust web-based studies? *American Psychologist, 59,* 93–104. doi: 10.1037/0003-066X.59.2.93

Plaud, J.J., Gaither, G.A., Hegstad, H.J., Rowan, L., & Devitt, M.K. (1999). Volunteer bias in human psychophysiological sexual research: To whom do our research results apply? *Journal of Sex Research, 36,* 171–179. doi: 10.1080/00224499909551982

The next pages are excerpts from two research articles using survey methods. You will read through these during class time and discuss.

More Eyes on the Prize

Variability in White Americans' Perceptions of Progress Toward Racial Equality

By Amanda B. Brodish, Paige C. Brazy, and Patricia G. Devine

STUDY 1

To extend Eibach and Ehrlinger's (2006) work in the ways described above, we expanded the assessment of perceptions of racial progress and developed separate and continuous measures of the tendency to anchor on the ideal future and the tendency to anchor on the past. We administered these measures to a large sample of White and non-White students. White participants in this sample also completed the Attitudes Towards Blacks Scale (ATB; Brigham, 1993), a measure of racial prejudice.

This study allows us to address four issues. First, we can examine the direction and magnitude of the relationship between anchoring on the past and anchoring on the ideal future. Second, we can examine mean level differences in perceptions of racial progress and reference points for understanding racial progress as a function of participant race. Third, we can replicate Eibach and Ehrlinger's (2006) finding that Whites' and non-Whites' differing perceptions of racial progress are mediated through the reference points used for understanding progress. Finally, we can explore variability in Whites' perceptions of racial progress as a function of prejudice and statistically test if anchoring on different reference points accounts for this relationship.

Before proceeding, we note that although there is likely meaningful variability in non-Whites'

perceptions of racial progress, our sample did not yield sufficient numbers of any one non-White group to explore this possibility. We return to this issue in the General Discussion.

Method

Participants

At the beginning of the semester, 1,128 introductory psychology students (58% female) participated in a large mass-testing session in exchange for course extra credit. Participants self-reported their race during this session (78% White, 3% Black, 15% Asian, and 5% Latino). Their average age was 19.34 years old (SD = 2.05, range = 18 to 57).

Measures

To assess perceptions of racial progress, we included five items that were rated on 7-point scales and were averaged to create an index of perceptions of racial progress (a = .77), such that higher scores reflect the tendency to perceive that more racial progress has been made. A sample item is "How much progress has been made toward equality for racial minorities in the US?"

Amanda B. Brodish, Paige C. Brazy, and Patricia G. Devine, "More Eyes on the Prize: Variability in White: Americans' Perceptions of Progress Toward Racial Equality," *Personality and Social Psychology Bulletin*, vol. 34, no. 4, pp. 516–517.

To assess anchoring on the past, we included two items assessing the extent to which participants anchor their judgment of racial progress on how far the US has come from the past. These items were rated on 7-point scales and were averaged to create an index of anchoring on the past (a = .63), such that higher scores reflect the tendency to more strongly anchor on how far the U.S. has come from the past. A sample item is "When I think about racial progress, I think about how much improvement the U.S. has made from the past."

To assess anchoring on the ideal future, we included two items assessing the extent to which participants anchor their judgment of racial progress on how far the U.S. has to go to achieve racial equality in the future. These items were rated on 7-point scales and were averaged to create an index of anchoring on the ideal future (a = .76), such that higher scores reflect the tendency to more strongly anchor how far the U.S. has to go. A sample item is "When I think about racial progress, I think about how much improvement the US has to make in the future." (See the appendix for the perceptions of racial progress, past and ideal future anchoring items.)

White participants also completed the ATB Scale. This scale includes 20 items that were rated on a scale ranging from 1 (strongly disagree) to 7 (strongly agree), reversed scored, as necessary, and averaged (a = .90) such that higher scores indicate more prejudice toward Blacks.[2] A sample item is "Generally, Blacks are not as smart as Whites."

Upon completion of the mass survey questionnaire, participants were provided with extra course credit; they were debriefed, in writing, later in the semester.

What Does it Mean to Be an American?

Patriotism, Nationalism, and American Identity
After 9/11

By Qiong Li and Marilynn B. Brewer

Design and Methods

A QUESTIONNAIRE survey was conducted during a 1-week period in late September 2001 with two respondent samples—one from students at Ohio State University, and the other a small community sample from Columbus, Ohio. The questionnaire was designed to assess American identification in terms of both patriotism and nationalism, perceptions of national cohesion and unity, and various attitudes related to tolerance of cultural diversity. A short paragraph inserted in the introduction to the questionnaire constituted the priming manipulation.

Participants

The university sample consisted of 148 college students (103 females and 45 males) who participated in this study in partial fulfillment of course requirements for their introductory psychology class. All were U.S. citizens. Of the total sample, 127 identified themselves as white Americans, 8 as African Americans, 6 as Asian Americans, 1 as Hispanic American, and 6 as "other."

The community sample consisted of 74 adults (32 females, 41 males, and 1 unspecified) who participated in the study voluntarily. The community respondents were recruited at a church and a restaurant in the local area and completed the questionnaires individually within that setting under the administration of a member of the research team. Although this was a convenience sample rather than a representative sample of the community, the two settings were selected to increase the overall diversity of our survey respondents. All participants were U.S. citizens; 56 of them identified as white Americans, 2 as African Americans, 8 as Asian Americans, 1 as Hispanic American, and 7 as "other."

Materials

The questionnaire consisted of two sections. The first section contained items designed to assess patriotism and nationalism, and the second section assessed diversity tolerance and affect toward outgroups. All items in this section were rated on a 7-point scale ranging from 1 (strongly disagree) to 7 (strongly agree).

Patriotism. Five items from the Kosterman and Feshbach (1989) patriotism scale were used to assess this aspect of identification with America: "I am proud to be an American," "I am emotionally attached to America and emotionally affected by its actions," "Although at times I may not agree with the government, my commitment to the U.S. always remains strong," "The fact I am an American is an important part of my identity," and "In general, I have very little respect for the American people" (reverse-scored).

Nationalism. Six items assessing nationalism were also taken from the Kosterman and Feshbach (1989) scale: "In view of America's moral and material superiority, it is only right that we should have the biggest say in deciding United Nations policy," "The first duty of every young American is to honor the national American history and heritage," "Other countries should try to make their government as much like ours as possible," "Foreign nations have done some very fine things but it takes America to do things in a big way," "It is really NOT important that the U.S. be number one in whatever it does" (reverse-scored), and "People should support their country even if the country is in the wrong."

Tolerance measures. Several items from the General Social Survey were adapted to assess attitudes toward cultural diversity and lifestyle diversity tolerance within the United States. These included four items assessing favorability toward multicultural values [e.g., "Ethnic minorities should be given government assistance to preserve their customs and traditions," "It is better for the country if different racial and ethnic groups adapt and blend into the larger society" (reverse-scored)] and three items assessing acceptance of lifestyle diversity (e.g., "homosexuality should be considered an acceptable lifestyle," "we should be more tolerant of people who choose to live according to their own standards, even if they are very different from our own"). These items were selected because they tap different aspects of acceptance of internal diversity and have been used frequently in national surveys.

For a more direct assessment of attitudes toward different cultural subgroups, respondents rated on a 7-point scale how close they felt to each of several social groups, including white Americans, black Americans, Asian Americans, and Muslim Americans.

Finally, as a measure of the inclusiveness of the representation of national identity, respondents indicated how important [on a 5-point scale ranging from 1 (not at all important) to 5 (extremely important)] each of several factors was to being "truly American." The factors rated included

"being born in the United States," "being able to speak English," and "being a Christian."

Priming Manipulation. A brief description that was inserted as part of the general instructions on the first page of the questionnaire was varied with the intent to prime alternative perceptions about the meaning of American identity. In the "core essence" priming condition, respondents read the following:

> The tragic events of September 11 have united Americans as never before in our generation. We have come to understand what we have in common as Americans. As a nation, our focus is on the core essence of what it means to be an American.

In the "common goal" priming condition, this paragraph was replaced with the following:

> The tragic events of September 11 have united Americans as never before in our generation. We now have a common purpose to fight terrorism in all of its forms and to work together to help those who were victims of this tragedy.

All other instructions were the same for both versions of the questionnaire.

Procedure

The university student participants completed the questionnaires in groups of 25 people over a 3-day period. The community sample respondents were administrated the questionnaire individually during the same period of time. For both samples, the alternative versions of the questionnaire were distributed randomly so that half of the respondents received the first priming manipulation and the other half the second.

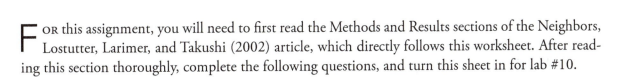

Survey Validation Worksheet

For this assignment, you will need to first read the Methods and Results sections of the Neighbors, Lostutter, Larimer, and Takushi (2002) article, which directly follows this worksheet. After reading this section thoroughly, complete the following questions, and turn this sheet in for lab #10.

1. What were the characteristics of the sample that was used to validate their gambling measures?

2. Based on the sample the survey was normed on (described in #1), do you think other populations would demonstrate the same responses to the survey items? Why or why not?

3. How were items for the Gambling Problem Index and the Gambling Readiness to Change Scale developed?

4. What types of statistics were reported in the article about the survey items?

5. What were the reliabilities reported for the following scales?

   Gambling Quantity Subscale:_____
   Gambling Problem Index: _____
   Gambling Readiness to Change Scale (composite): _____

6. What was the correlation between the Gambling Quantity Subscale and the Gambling Problem Index?

7. Based on what is reported, do you think the measures in this study are valid? What weaknesses (if any) do you think they have?

8. If you were to conduct a study measuring gambling behaviors, would you feel comfortable using the measures reported in this study? Why or why not? What might you change about them?

Measuring Gambling Outcomes Among College Students

By Clayton Neighbors, Ty W. Lostutter, Mary E. Larimer, and Ruby Y. Takushi

METHOD

Participants

PARTICIPANTS included 560 (204 men and 347 women) college students enrolled in undergraduate psychology courses at a large northwestern university in the U.S. (nine participants did not indicate gender). Participants were recruited via sign up sheets inviting the participation of all students "who had ever gambled at least once in their life, even if just bingo or lottery." Students received extra course credit for participation. The average age of participants was 19.24 years (SD = 1.77). Ethnicity was 58.7% Caucasian, 34.1% Asian/Asian American, 1.7% Hispanic/Latino, 1.3% Black/African American and 4.2% other. The sample included 26.0% fraternity (n = 51) and sorority (n = 92) members. Participants were freshman (55.3%), sophomores (28.1%), juniors (11.3%), and seniors (4.9%). Participants included individuals who gambled non-problematically (83.9%; SOGS < 3), sub-clinical problem gamblers (9.8%; SOGS = 3 or 4) and probable pathological gamblers (6.3%; SOGS = 5 or higher). The university is located in a community in which there is ample access to gambling venues for college students, including six Tribal/Indian casinos and 1,842 active operator licenses in the three county area surrounding the university.

Procedure

Participants completed all measures, which were presented in the same order, in small groups, with no communication between participants. Participants were urged to answer all items honestly and were reminded that all answers would remain anonymous. All measures and procedures were reviewed and approved by the departmental human subjects committee. Following the assessment, participants were debriefed and thanked for their participation.

Measures

The Gambling Problem Index (GPI; Appendix A) consisted of 20 items and was constructed for this research. The GPI was closely modeled after the Rutgers Alcohol Problem Index (RAPI; White & Labouvie, 1989), an established measure designed to assess alcohol related problems. For each item respondents were asked to indicate, on a 5-point scale (never, one to two, three to five, six to ten, and more than ten times), how many times during the previous six months they experienced a negative consequence while gambling or as a result of gambling. The GPI score was calculated as the sum of items in which participants reported experiencing the gambling related consequence, at least once, during the previous six months.

The Gambling Readiness to Change Scale (GRTC; Appendix B) was constructed for this

Clayton Neighbors, Ty W. Lostutter, Mary E. Larimer, and Ruby Y. Takushi, "Measuring Gambling Outcomes Among College Students," *Journal of Gambling Studies*, vol. 18, no. 4, pp. 342–348. Copyright © 2002 by Springer Science+Business Media. Reprinted with permission.

research and was modeled after the alcohol Readiness To Change questionnaire (Rollnick et al., 1992), which is based on Prochaska and DiClemente's (1986) stages-of-change model. The GRTC is a 9-item scale with three items measuring each of three stages: precontemplation, contemplation, and action. Respondents indicate the extent to which they agree with the statement presented in each item, from 1 (strongly disagree) to 5 (strongly agree). The GRTC may be scored in three ways according to the specific aims of the research in which it is used. An overall composite of readiness to change consists of weighting the precontemplation items (–2), contemplation items (1), and action items (2), and taking the mean of all weighted items. Alternatively, separate scores for precontemplation, contemplation, and action can be derived by taking the mean of the items corresponding to each subscale. A third alternative is to categorize individuals as precontemplators, contemplators, or in the action stage according to their highest subscale score. Results described herein are geared toward the first two alternatives.

The Gambling Quantity and Perceived Norms Scale (GQPN, Appendix C) includes six items (items 4–9) assessing money spent gambling and was designed as a gambling quantity measure. Respondents are asked how much money they have won and lost from gambling over the previous month and year. Responses are coded on 10-point scales with anchors ranging from less than $5 to more than $1,000 for wins and losses per month and $25 to more than $2,000 for wins and losses per year. One item (item 1) measures disposable income and allows for statistical control of relevant income. The quantity scale is scored as the mean of the six expenditure items residualized on the disposable income item. The GQPN includes a single frequency item (item 2) with responses coded on a 10-point scale from "never" to "every day." The GQPN also includes a perceived norms scale (items 10–13), which was included for other purposes and is not discussed further.

The South Oaks Gambling Screen (SOGS; Lesieur & Blume, 1987) is a widely used 20-item self-administered screening questionnaire designed to identify probable pathological gamblers. The SOGS correlates highly with the DSM-III-R and DSM-IV with demonstrated validity and reliability among university students (Beaudoin & Cox, 1999; Lesieur et al., 1991; Ladouceur et al., 1994). Sample scored items include "Have you ever felt like you would like to stop gambling but didn't think you could?" and "Have you ever lost time from work (or school due to gambling?" A score of five or more on the SOGS has been used to identify probable pathological gamblers. Previous researchers have identified individuals scoring three or four on the SOGS as sub-clinical problem gamblers (Dube et al., 1996; Lesieur et al., 1991; Volberg & Steadman, 1988). The SOGS also includes an item related to frequency of various types of gambling, from 0 (never) to once a week or more (2). Consistent with previous research (e.g., Moore & Ohtsuka, 1999), we created a gambling frequency index based on this item by taking the mean of reported frequency for each type of gambling activity.

The 20 Questions of Gamblers Anonymous (GA20) consists of 20 dichotomous items (yes/no) describing situations and behaviors characteristic of problem gamblers and has previously demonstrated good reliability and convergent validity (Ursua & Uribelarrea, 1998). Sample items include, "Have you ever sold anything to finance gambling?", "Were you reluctant to use "gambling money" for normal expenditures?", and "Did gambling make you careless of the welfare of yourself or your family?" The GA20 was scored as the sum of endorsed items.

The Gambling Attitudes and Beliefs Scale (GABS; Breen & Zuckerman, 1999) assesses general attitudes toward gambling. The GABS focuses on cognitive factors related to gambling and includes 35 items to which respondents report the extent to which they agree, from 1 (strongly disagree) to 4 (strongly agree). Sample items include "Some people can bring bad luck

Table 1
Means and Standard Deviations for Gambling Outcomes

	Overall (n = 560)		Men (n = 204)		Women (n = 347)	
SOGS	1.29	(1.81)	1.67	(2.14)	1.06	(1.56)
GA20	2.53	(2.43)	3.07	(2.50)	2.23	(2.37)
SOGS Freq	0.58	(0.29)	0.67	(0.30)	0.53	(0.27)
GABS	2.27	(0.38)	2.36	(0.38)	2.22	(0.38)
Quantity	1.66	(0.95)	1.83	(1.06)	1.42	(0.84)
GQPN Freq	3.32	(1.29)	3.77	(1.38)	3.05	(1.17)
GPI	1.58	(2.77)	2.19	(2.98)	1.34	(2.61)

Note: SOGS refers to the South Oaks Gambling Screen. GA20 refers to the Gamblers Anonymous 20 Questions. SOGS Freq refers to the SOGS frequency index. GABS refers to the Gambling Attitudes and Beliefs Scale. GQPN Freq refers to the frequency item on the GQPN. GPI refers to Gambling Problems Index. Standard deviations are in parentheses. All gender differences were significant at $p < .001$.

to other people," and "If I have lost my bets recently, my luck is bound to change." The GABS was scored as the mean of all items. Higher scores indicate pro-gambling attitudes and beliefs.

RESULTS

Gambling Prevalence

Table 1 presents overall, and by gender, means and standard deviations of gambling outcome measures. Problem gambling was consistently more evident among men than women. Using the SOGS to categorize gamblers as non-problem (SOGS < 3), sub-clinical problem (SOGS = 3 or 4), and probable pathological (SOGS = 5 or higher) revealed that men were more likely than women to be classified as probable pathological gamblers (10.78% vs. 3.75%; $x^2 = 10.70$, p < .01) but men and women did not differ in likelihood of being classified as sub-clinical problem gamblers (10.78% vs. 9.22%, $x^2 < 1$, p = .55).

Reliability and Validity

Gambling Quantity and Frequency. The gambling quantity subscale of the GQPN demonstrated good reliability (alpha = .89). The six quantity items (amount won and lost) loaded highly on a single factor (factor loadings ranged

from .77 to .85) and accounted for 65.3% of the variance among these items. In order to control for differences in disposable income we residualized the mean of the six quantity items on the disposable income item. References to the gambling quantity measure refer to this residualized variable. Correlations with other gambling outcome measures ranged from .39 to .61 providing convergent validity for the gambling quantity measure. The gambling frequency item also demonstrated good convergent validity. Correlations with other gambling outcomes ranged from .30 to .54. The GQPN frequency item was moderately correlated with the SOGS frequency index and was similarly associated with other gambling outcome measures (see Table 2).

The Gambling Problem Index. The GPI was internally consistent (alpha = .84) and demonstrated good convergent validity. The GPI, like the RAPI upon which it was modeled, was conceptualized as a general index of problems manifested as a result of gambling behavior, hence we were primarily interested in testing the internal consistency of the instrument and less concerned with its specific factor structure. The GPI, however, displayed similar factor structure to the RAPI, with 6 factors having Eigenvalues above one, whereas the RAPI produced 5 factors with Eigenvalues above one. Convergent validity of the gambling problem index was established

Table 2
Convergent Validity: Correlations Among Gambling Outcome Indices

	SOGS	GA20	SOGS Freq	GABS	Quantity	GQPN Freq	GPI
SOGS	—	.55	.30	.35	.58	.30	.42
GA20	.55	—	.43	.56	.61	.44	.52
SOGS Freq	.30	.43	—	.41	.39	.42	.46
GABS	.35	.56	.41	—	.47	.36	.35
Quantity	.58	.61	.39	.47	—	.54	.48
GQPN Freq	.30	.44	.42	.36	.54	—	.36
GPI	.42	.52	.46	.35	.48	.36	—

Note. N's ranged from 554 to 560 depending on missing data. SOGS refers to the South Oaks Gambling Screen. GA20 refers to the Gamblers Anonymous 20 Questions. SOGS Freq refers to the SOGS frequency index. GABS refers to the Gambling Attitudes and Beliefs Scale. GQPN Freq refers to the frequency item on the GQPN. GPI refers to Gambling Problems Index. All correlations are significant at $p < .0001$.

Table 3
Principal Components of Gambling Readiness to Change

Factor Number	Eigenvalue	Explained Variance	Cumulative Variance
1	3.77 (2.20)	41.9% (24.4%)	41.9% (24.4%)
2	1.29 (2.02)	14.3% (22.4%)	56.2% (46.8%)
3	1.01 (1.85)	11.2% (20.6%)	67.5% (67.5%)

Note. Varimax rotated values are in parentheses.

through correlations with other gambling outcome measures, which ranged from .39 to .61 (see Table 2).

The Gambling Readiness to Change Scale. Because the GRTC scale is only appropriate for measuring readiness to change among individuals who gamble at least moderately, and thus might have reason to change their gambling behavior, only individuals scoring three or higher on the SOGS were included in analyses of readiness to change.[1] In evaluating the reliability and validity of the GRTC, we began by testing the assumption that the three stages (precontemplation, contemplation, and action) were evident and distinguishable. Principal components analysis revealed strong support for a three-factor solution, with three factors having Eigenvalues above 1, accounting for 67.5% of the total variance (see Table 3). Rotated factor loadings (Varimax rotation) revealed that the contemplation items

loaded strongly on Factor 1, the action items loaded on Factor 2, and the precontemplation items loaded on Factor 3 (see Table 4). None of the items exhibited cross-loadings greater than .35.

The GRTC scale demonstrated satisfactory reliability for the composite scale (alpha = .81), and each of the three subscales, with alphas of .64, .80, and .74 for precontemplation, contemplation, and action respectively. Convergent validity was established by examining correlations of the readiness to change composite, and each of its sub-scales with gambling outcome measures. Alpha levels were adjusted for multiple comparisons using Bonferroni correction. As expected, results suggested a simplex structure with more problematic gambling associated with greater readiness to change one's gambling behavior (see Table 3).

Lab #10

Purpose:
- The purpose of this lab is to learn how to locate and administer surveys.
- Students will also learn how to use computerized survey programs.

Objectives:
- Receive final hypothesis from your instructor.
- Discuss survey validation worksheet based on Neighbors's article.
- Learn about MediaLab and/or other computerized survey programs, and practice using it/them. Also, learn about best practices for conducting online surveys by discussing the following section entitled Administering Computerized Surveys.
- Operationalize hypothesis using survey method.
- Locate possibly surveys for use in your study, and learn tips for searching for surveys in PsycINFO.

Homework:
- Identify a survey that you may use in your study. Complete summary of survey homework.
- Complete the IAT exercise, and bring completed worksheet to the next lab.
- Study for quiz on labs #7–10.

Administering Computerized Surveys

IN the not-so-distant past, virtually all surveys were administered via pencil and paper. Of course, you still have the option of doing this today, but be aware that it requires significant time, effort, and cost on your part. For example, with such surveys, you must physically put them in the hands of participants yourself. Moreover, all data collected will need to be entered into a statistical program by hand, in order to analyze it. If you collect a large amount of data and/or ask a lot of questions, this can be burdensome. Not only that, but it must be done slowly—and with great care—to ensure that all of the data are entered correctly; otherwise, you risk coming to the wrong conclusions (and just one wrong piece of data can throw off all of your results!).

Fortunately, administering surveys has become easier in recent years with the development of computerized programs that can collect data for you. These programs can save you a significant amount of time—not to mention the fact that they substantially reduce the risk of incorrect data entry, because they automatically create an electronic data file that can be directly analyzed by a variety of statistical programs.

You have two basic options for administering a computerized survey. First, you could have participants come into your research lab and complete it in person. For administering a survey like this, many researchers use programs such as MediaLab. If your university has a license

for MediaLab, your instructor will go through a demonstration of this program with you today. If you do not have access to MediaLab, but would like to try it out for future reference, please visit the following website: http://www.empirisoft.com/Download.aspx

Second, if you do not have lab space to run participants through your study, you could post your survey on-line instead. One of the advantages of on-line research is that you tend to capture much more diversity in your sample than you can get simply by recruiting fellow college students. You can create your survey through a number of companies, including SurveyMonkey.com, Psychdata.com, and Qualtrics.com (of course, there are many other options available, but these are among the most widely used by psychologists). If your university has a license for using one of these programs, your instructor will show you how to use it today.

If you decide to use an on-line survey in order to collect your data for this course, we have listed a few important pointers below. Please be sure to refer to these pages, if and when the time comes.

—WHERE TO POST: You can post links to your survey virtually anywhere (e.g., on-line message boards or forums, Facebook pages, CraigsList, etc.). Many of these sites will allow you to post ads for free, but others will charge. Please keep in mind that you will face certain selection biases if you recruit through "specialty" websites. That is, be sure to think about the demographic features of the people who visit those websites, and how that could potentially influence your results (e.g., how are Facebook users different from the rest of the population in terms of age, education level, socioeconomic status, etc.).

—FOLLOW PROPER ETIQUETTE: If you elect to post a link to your survey on a message board as a means of recruiting participants, e-mail the website's moderator first to ask for permission. At the very least, make sure to read the site's rules prior to posting, to ensure that requests for participation are appropriate and permissible. People who violate these rules may have their postings removed, but they can also create hostility toward on-line researchers in general, making it more difficult for other researchers to obtain participants in the future.

—MINIMIZE SURVEY SIZE: If you are asking people to complete your survey without compensating them for their time, it is vital that you make sure to only ask the questions that are absolutely necessary. The shorter the survey is, the greater the likelihood that participants will complete the entire thing. If it is too long, you might end up restricting your sample size and/or finding that many participants stop before getting to the end. For this reason, it is also important to "front-load" your survey—that is, put the most important questions first, and leave everything else for later.

Operationalization of Hypothesis: Survey Method

C OMPLETE the following exercise in your group during the lab. You will present your answers in front of the class, and then have a discussion. Then, submit the form to your lab instructor.

Names of individuals in your group:

1. Original hypothesis:

2. If you were to use a survey method for your study, how would you operationalize your hypothesis?

3. Has this method ever been used to test hypotheses similar to yours? How? To what effect?

4. What are some possible benefits of using this method to test your hypothesis?

5. What are some possible limitations of using this method to test your hypothesis?

6. What ethical issues (if any) might you have if you used a survey method to test your hypothesis? How might you overcome these issues? (*Hint: Have any other studies had to address these issues?*)

Survey Summary
Homework

For this assignment, you will need to locate a survey that your group might consider using for your lab project (see the next page for help on how to do this). As a group, select a survey, and then find the original article that reports the survey items and reliability and validation information. If the original cannot be found, then locate another article that reports this information. Read through the article, and then answer the following questions. Please write your responses below, and turn this sheet in at the next lab meeting. Be sure to attach the original article that you got your information from.

1. Which survey did you select?

2. What is the APA citation for the article that reports on the measure?

3. What are the characteristics of the sample that was used to validate the survey?

4. Based on the sample the survey was normed on (described in #3), do you think other populations would demonstrate the same responses to the survey items? Why or why not? (Try conducting a PsycINFO literature search to see if other studies have validated the measure with other samples.)

5. How were items for the survey developed?

6. What types of statistics were reported in the article about the survey items?

7. What is the reliability for the survey?

8. How was the survey validated?

9. Based on what you now know about this measure, do you think it would be appropriate to use in your lab study this semester? Why or why not?

10. Does the survey measure everything that you want to know for the purposes of your study? What is missing?

Locating a Survey Using PsycINFO

IN order to search for articles concerning a specific topic and testing, type your topic into the first search box (e.g., attachment). In the corresponding "Select a Field (Optional)" box, you can leave it blank. In the second search box, type the number 2220, and in its corresponding Field box, select "CC Classification." This type of search is often a good first step when looking for surveys. It will pull up a lot of articles on your topic and help you to identify some different measures that might be of interest to you.

Once you have found a measure you want to use, you will often want to locate other articles that have used it as well in order to get additional information on validity and reliability, and to see modifications or changes that have occurred (sometimes measures are updated over time or modified to fit specific study purposes.) In order to search for articles in which a specific test or measure was given to participants, type the measure's name into the first search box (e.g., Adult Attachment Questionnaire), and in the corresponding Field box, select "TM Tests & Measure."

Alternatively, you can do a search for articles that discuss the specific measure you are interested in by typing the measure's name in the first search box (e.g., Adult Attachment Questionnaire.) In the corresponding Field box, select "SU Subjects."

PRIMING AND AUTOMATICITY PROCEDURES

Name: _____

IAT Exercise

For this project, you will take a test of implicit associations on-line. As we will discuss in class, people have implicit associations with a variety of things. By "implicit," we mean that people are not aware that they have (or are exhibiting) those associations.

To complete this project, you will need access to the Internet with a computer that can support Java applets. Most computers are fine, but you will need to plan accordingly. Go to the following website: https://implicit.harvard.edu/implicit//demo/

*After reading the information, go to "demonstration tests."

* Choose one of the implicit association tests.

After you finish one IAT, try at least one additional IAT. Feel free to do as many as you want. Report on your experience:

1. Which tests did you take? _____

_____

2. Were the test(s) results consistent with your conscious attitudes and beliefs? If not, how were they different? _____

_____

_____

_____

_____

3. Why do you think you obtained the results that you did? _____

_____

_____

_____

_____

_____

4. What do you think the IAT is showing? Your "true" attitude; an attitude you probably have, but are trying to change; an old association you thought had changed; cultural associations; something else?

_____

_____

_____

_____

5. Did completing the IAT make you think about stereotypes and prejudice any differently than you did before? If yes, how? If no, why not? _____

_____

_____

_____

_____

6. Now go back to the IAT website and take one of the tests over again. Try to change your results (but still take the test in a valid manner—e.g., don't close your eyes). What did you try? Were you successful? What does this make you think of the IAT? _____

_____

_____

_____

_____

_____

Lab #11

Purpose:

- Learn about priming and automaticity procedures.

Objectives:

- Take quiz on labs #7–10.
- Review the following section entitled Priming and Automaticity Procedures and discuss the rationale for using these methods in social psychological research.
- Learn about different types of research questions that can be answered with this procedure.
- Learn about a variety of priming (conceptual, supraliminal, subliminal) and automaticity techniques used in social psychological research.
- Learn about Inquisit software and other methods of measuring automatic responding.
    - If your university does not carry a license for Inquisit, a free trial demonstration of this software is available at: http://www.millisecond.com/
    - Alternatively, you can simply preview the functions and capability of Inquisit by consulting the demonstrations available at: http://www.millisecond.com/products/demos/
- Evaluate the IAT measure.
- Read Method sections from two published articles using priming or automaticity procedures.
- Operationalize hypothesis using priming or automaticity measures.

Homework:

- Complete study rationale worksheet.
- Submit an outline for your paper.

Priming and Automaticity Procedures

PRIMING and automaticity research are both concerned with how the activation of certain mental representations and procedures can affect our psychological responses in ways outside of conscious awareness. More specifically, **priming** occurs when situational factors trigger a certain mental representation that, in turn, alters our subsequent perceptions of events and/or our behaviors (e.g., seeing a picture of a pleasant stimulus, such as puppies or kittens, may put us in a positive mood, and that may lead us to be friendlier to other people). In contrast, **automaticity** is a related construct that refers to individually held mental representations that allow us to carry out various tasks non-consciously (e.g., reading, driving, forming impressions of others). Priming and automaticity research both provide us with some sense of the internal processes that guide our attitudes and behaviors.

There are several forms that priming can take in social psychological research. One is **conceptual priming**, which involves activating a specific mental representation in one task and then observing how participants respond during a subsequent task. In order for this to work, the link between the activated representation and the follow-up task must not be consciously recognizable by the participant. In conceptual priming, mental representations can either be activated subliminally or supraliminally. Subliminal priming occurs when the activating stimulus is presented completely outside of conscious awareness. For example, a picture or word may be presented on a computer screen for a fraction of a second followed by a pattern mask (another picture or word that overwrites the prime to ensure that the primed stimulus does not reach the level of conscious awareness). In studies that employ subliminal priming, participants are usually given follow-up questions after the prime to confirm that they did not consciously recognize the stimulus. In comparison, supraliminal priming occurs when the activating stimulus is presented consciously, but participants are not aware that they are being primed. For instance, one of the most common forms of supraliminal priming is the scrambled sentence task, in which participants are given a seemingly ordinary language task. Specifically, participants must take a series of sentences in which the words are out of order and rearrange all of the words so as to form grammatically correct sentences. Embedded within some of the scrambled sentences are certain key words that represent the construct(s) the researcher wishes to prime. In supraliminal priming studies, participants are usually probed for suspicion to ensure that they did not recognize the true purpose of the study.

An alternative to conceptual priming is **mindset priming**, which involves getting participants to act upon a mental representation first, and then observing the extent to which that same mindset "carries over" into subsequent tasks. As one common example of this, gain/loss mindsets are often primed in social psychological studies (Rothman, Bartels, Wlaschin, & Salovey, 2006). That is, some participants may be instructed to think of a given behavior in terms of the benefits of action (i.e., gain perspective), whereas others might be instructed to think of the same behavior in terms of the costs of inaction (i.e., loss perspective). After considering one behavior in this light, participants may then be given a new behavior to consider, in which the same mindset will presumably prevail because participants have already been primed to use it.

Automaticity research methods can take several forms as well, but much of the published research you will see in social psychology tends to focus on processing efficiency (e.g., how quickly does a given reaction occur?). The more automated a given process is, the faster it happens—and this processing should occur just as quickly regardless of one's level of attention because conscious attention is not required. Measures of automaticity often rely upon both reaction time and error rates, such as the **Implicit Association Test (IAT)** (Greenwald, McGhee, & Schwartz, 1998). The IAT tests the degree to which we hold positive or negative associations with various social objects. In perhaps the most well-known variant of the IAT, participants are given an online task in which they are asked to categorize Black and White faces, as well as positive and negative descriptive terms. When participants have an easier time associating one racial category with negative terms and a harder time associating that same category with positive terms (as evidenced by both reaction time and

error rates), psychologists often take this as evidence of holding an unconscious bias.

The value of priming and automaticity measures is that they can give us a glimpse into how automatic and non-conscious processing occur and the effects they can have. This is important to study for a few reasons, with one of them being that much of our everyday processing is relatively automatic (e.g., consider how little thought you need to put into driving your car to work or back home—many of us can do this on "autopilot"). However, while all of this automatic processing is great for efficiency, it does come at a cost. For instance, automatic processing can sometimes lead us to rely too heavily on stereotypes in forming impressions of other people. As evidenced by the widespread usage of the IAT and other such tests, the origins and effects of non-conscious biases have become the focus of a growing amount of research in this area over the past two decades.

References

Greenwald, A. G., McGhee, D. E., & Schwartz, J. L. (1998). Measuring individual differences in implicit cognition: The implicit association test. *Journal of Personality and Social Psychology, 74*, 1464. doi: 10.1037/0022–3514.74.6.1464

Rothman, A. J., Bartels, R. D., Wlaschin, J., & Salovey, P. (2006). The strategic use of gain- and loss-framed messages to promote healthy behavior: How theory can inform practice. *Journal of Communication, 56*(s1), S202–S220. doi: 10.1111/j.1460-2466.2006.00290.x

The next pages are excerpts from two research articles using priming or automaticity methods. You will read through these during class time and discuss.

Narcissism Beyond Gestalt and Awareness

The Name Letter Effect

By Jozef M. Nuttin

METHOD

THE two experiments to be reported below were basically similar qua stimulus presentation, yoked design and instructions. For each subject a unique ad hoc stimulus list (see Figure 1) of printed capital letter pairs (or triads) was prepared. Each list contained all the letters of the family name and first name of one subject. These name letters, one per row, were printed in spelling order from bottom to top. On each line, the name letter was randomly assigned to the left, (middle) or right position. To each name letter one (or two) not-name letter(s) were added, selected in a standardized manner from the remaining letters which did not belong to the name concealed in each particular stimulus list. In some conditions the letters Q, X, Y and Z, with very low frequency in Dutch, were never used as not-name letters.

In the yoked design, subjects were arranged in experimental pairs on a random basis (except that the names of the yoked members did not share common syllables). The crucial feature was that both members A and B of each pair had to evaluate an identical set of two stimulus lists, one containing the name of subject A and one containing the name of subject B. Thus, within each yoked pair, all stimulus characteristics were kept constant, except for the manipulated "within subject" factor of mere belongingness to self of the set of name letter stimuli.

The oral instructions given by the experimenter to each isolated subject aimed at dispelling any task apprehensions and at achieving a mental relaxation so as to maximally avoid free associations, thinking or reasoning during the task: "What I'm about to ask you is very simple. I'll show you a series of printed figures, symbols or drawings which will look very familiar to you. I do not tell you yet which kind of figures they are going to be, because I do not want you to prepare your answers beforehand. As a matter of fact, I am only interested in your first, spontaneous and immediate reactions, which I expect you to give as fast as possible. As soon as I show you the lists of figures, please do not hesitate and do not ponder on their shape, meaning or format. Let your choices only be governed by your general positive (negative) feelings towards the printed figures, drawings or symbols. Although the task is by itself very simple, it might however become somewhat more difficult when I urge you to make your choices without thinking. So please, do your best to stop all thinking and simply try to feel which symbol is most attractive in each pair (or group of three); (which symbol is least attractive in each pair); (which are the 2 least attractive symbols in each group of three)." Each subject was then given either two lists of letter pairs or two lists of letter triads and was asked

Jozef M. Nuttin, "Narcissism Beyond Gestalt and Awareness: The Name Letter Effect," *European Journal of Social Psychology,* vol. 15, no. 3, pp. 354–356. Copyright © 1985 by John Wiley & Sons, Inc. Reprinted with permission.

Zajonc Robert pairs	Rijsman John pairs	Zajonc Robert triads	Rijsman John triads
T D	N B	D W T	B V N
R F	H C	F D R	C W H
E G	O D	G F E	D B O
H B	E J	H B G	E J C
O I	N F	O I H	N F D
K R	G A	K I R	G E A
C L	M K	C L K	M K F
M N	L S	M N L	L S G
P O	P J	P O M	P J K
J S	I T	J S P	I T L
A U	R U	U A S	U R P
V Z		Z V U	

Figure 1. Example of name stimulus lists of letter pairs and triads constructed for fictitious subjects named Zajonc Robert and Rijsman John (without QXYZ as not-name letters). The arrows in the first stimulus list, starting at the bottom with the initial Z of the family name Zajonc, are merely given in order to help the reader to discover the concealed names. These arrows were, of course, omitted in the stimulus lists given to the experimental subjects

either to encircle as spontaneously and fast as possible the most attractive letter in each letter pair or triad or to cross out the least attractive letter in each letter pair or the two least attractive letters in each letter triad.

The dependent measure was the proportion of name letters chosen (or not rejected) in each stimulus list. The proportion is 1 when, for each letter pair (or triad) of a list, a subject prefers (or does not reject) the name letter and is 0 when, for each pair (or triad) (s)he prefers (or does not reject) a not-name letter. The prediction tested is that the average proportion of name letters chosen (or not rejected) in the own name lists will be higher than in the yoked partners' name lists. For the analysis of the results, the names are treated as random cases, each having two repeated measures: one as own name and one as partner's name. It should be noted that the hypothesis is tested in a conservative way. The names of yoked subjects do have common letters (the two names used in Figure 1 have 5 common letters: J, O, N, A, and R). If each subject prefers (or does not reject) the common "own name letters" in each of the two lists, these choices do not contribute to the predicted difference, although they might in fact be determined by the crucial experimental factor "mere belongingness to self."

Automatic Attitudes and Alcohol

Does Implicit Liking Predict Drinking?

By B. Keith Payne, Olesya Govorun, and Nathan L. Arbuckle

STUDY 1: TASTE TEST

THE aim of our first experiment was to test whether implicit attitudes toward beer as measured by the AMP could predict beer-drinking behaviour. We first measured participants' attitudes toward beer using the AMP. We then arranged a taste test, and asked participants to choose whether they preferred to taste a new brand of beer or bottled water. Of interest was which beverage participants chose to drink, and whether this choice was associated with AMP scores.

Method

Participants

Forty-three volunteers (26 men and 17 women) were recruited in the Ohio State University student centre to participate in an experiment on taste preferences. Participation was limited to individuals 21 years of age or older because the study was related to alcohol. Volunteers were paid four dollars.

Materials

Affect misattribution procedure. The AMP was constructed identically to the procedure reported by Payne et al. (2005). At the beginning of the task, participants were told that various Chinese characters would appear on a computer screen, and that they would evaluate each item on pleasantness. Participants were instructed to press the key labelled "pleasant" if they found a character to be more pleasant than the average Chinese pictograph, and to press the key labelled "unpleasant" if they found a character to be less pleasant than average. Participants were told that each character would be preceded by an image of water, beer, or a grey square, and that these images could bias their judgements of the pictographs. As part of the task instructions, participants were told that their task was to try their "absolute best" not to let their like or dislike for the images influence their judgement of the characters.

Twelve colour photographs of beer and drinking water served as primes. Six judges rated the visual appeal of 20 alcohol photos and 20 water photos on a 7-point scale. They were asked to rate the attractiveness of the drinks without regard to whether they liked the drink featured. The 12 beer photos and 12 water photos were selected from these to be matched on visual attractiveness so that there was no difference between beer and water items. On each trial, the prime was presented in the middle of the screen for 75 ms and was replaced by a blank screen for a 125 ms interval (Figure 1, third panel). A Chinese pictograph then appeared for 100 ms and was followed by a pattern mask, which consisted of a white and black pattern

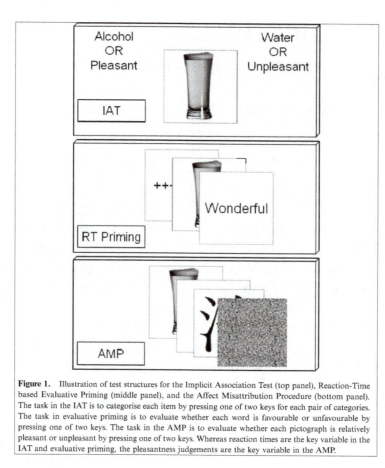

Figure 1. Illustration of test structures for the Implicit Association Test (top panel), Reaction-Time based Evaluative Priming (middle panel), and the Affect Misattribution Procedure (bottom panel). The task in the IAT is to categorise each item by pressing one of two keys for each pair of categories. The task in evaluative priming is to evaluate whether each word is favourable or unfavourable by pressing one of two keys. The task in the AMP is to evaluate whether each pictograph is relatively pleasant or unpleasant by pressing one of two keys. Whereas reaction times are the key variable in the IAT and evaluative priming, the pleasantness judgements are the key variable in the AMP.

of "noise." The mask stayed on the screen until participants made a response. Participants completed 72 trials, in which each of the 12 beer primes and 12 water primes was presented twice, and the grey square was presented 24 times. Seventy-two unique Chinese characters were used as targets and were randomly paired with the primes. At the end of the task, participants were asked if they spoke Chinese or Japanese so that those who did could be excluded from analysis (because the characters would not be ambiguous for them). In this sample, no participants were eliminated.

Procedure

Participants were recruited to participate from a table in a public area of the University student centre. Volunteers were escorted to a quiet testing room in the student centre for the actual experiment. Participants first completed the AMP on a laptop computer. They were then escorted into a different room for a taste test. They were informed that they could sample either a new brand of premium water or a new brand of beer. Non-alcoholic beer was used, but participants were not informed about the alcohol content until the end of the study.

Participants were asked to indicate to the experimenter which beverage they would like to sample. Participants reported how much they liked the beverage they sampled on a scale from 1 (not at all) to 10 (very much). Participants who chose beer were asked to estimate its alcohol content as a way to ensure that participants were not suspicious about the beverage options. They rated the beer from 1 (no alcohol content) to 10 (very high alcohol content). Participants were then fully debriefed and paid for their participation.

Operationalization of Hypothesis: Priming or Automaticity Method

COMPLETE the following exercise in your group during the lab. You will present your answers in front of the class, and then have a discussion. Afterward, submit the form to your lab instructor.

Names of individuals in your group:

1. Original hypothesis:

2. If you were to use a priming or "automatic" method for your study, how would you operationalize your hypothesis? Has this method ever been used to test hypotheses similar to yours? How? To what effect?

3. What are some possible benefits of using this method to test your hypothesis?

4. What are some possible limitations of using this method to test your hypothesis?

5. What ethical issues (if any) might you have if you used a priming or "automatic" method to test your hypothesis? How might you overcome these issues? (*Hint: Have any other studies had to address these issues?*)

Study Rationale Worksheet

Now that you have settled on the hypothesis that you will be testing in your experiment this semester, it is now important to develop a strong rationale as to *why* you are going to test that particular hypothesis. This rationale is used to build a case as to why your study is important; what new information your study will add to the research area; and to help assess whether the risks involved in your research are outweighed by the benefits of the knowledge that will be learned.

Therefore, before writing the Introduction for your paper and your forms for mock IRB approval, you will need to develop a strong rationale for your study. Your assignment will be to write a short paper answering the following questions. If you are not able to answer these questions, you will have a very hard time providing a good rationale for your project, and your grade on the project will suffer. Take some time and think hard about these four questions:

1. What was the original theory or hypothesis that you based your study on? Describe it in four or more sentences.
2. What are the limitations of this theory or research that you hope your study will address? Describe at least one.
3. What theoretical or empirical evidence do you have to believe that your new hypothesis might be supported? Provide evidence using APA-cited references. This answer should be at least four to six sentences long.
4. Why is your hypothesis important? What are the larger implications? This should be at least four to six sentences in length as well.

Please type your responses using double spacing and 12-point font, and turn your papers in at the next lab meeting. Print out an additional copy for yourself, because you will be discussing this sheet in your lab group at the next meeting.

Feedback on Drafts of Paper

NOTE: For the rest of the class, you will be receiving feedback on drafts of your research paper. Your final paper **must** be APA formatted, so the feedback that you receive on these early drafts will help to ensure that you will not lose points for failing to use this formatting style correctly. It is in your own best interest to complete these assignments on time, to ensure a good grade on your final paper.

The following table addresses the criteria you should heed in putting together your final paper. Please refer to it as you write your paper throughout the semester:

Section	Part/Issue
Title Page	Be sure to include one!
Abstract	Mention Problem/Hypothesis
	Mention Participants
	Mention Method/Design
	Address Results/Conclusions
Introduction	Introduce Main Topic/Problem
	Discuss & Integrate Relevant Studies
	Transition from Literature to Current Study
	Identify Independent and Dependent Variables
	Hypothesis(es) Stated
Method	Participants
	Research Design/Materials/Procedure
Results	Summary of Descriptive Statistics
	Summary of Inferential Statistics
	Reference to Figure/Table
Discussion	Restatement of Purpose/Hypothesis(es)
	Integration of Past Studies
	Explanation of Results
	Discussion of Strengths and Limitations
	Implications or Applications of the Research
	Future Research Directions
	Summary Statement/Conclusions
Reference Page	All Citations Present
Table & Figure	At Least One Table/Figure Present
APA Style/Format	Headers, Titles, Spacing, References, Citations, etc.
	APA Style, Grammar, and Spelling

For the Next Lab: Outline of Paper

For this assignment, you are to start developing an outline of your paper, using APA format. We know that you have not done a thorough literature review yet. However, you are able to start creating an outline of your paper. This is purely for you to get used to the formatting style; we can correct things early.

Start by consulting the APA manual, or one of the APA formatting websites mentioned previously. The APA manual has an example of a one-experiment paper, which is what you will be writing. For your outline draft, we want you to create a Word document with the essential sections, headers, etc., that would appear in your paper.

Thus, you would have a title page with a title (you can make anything up at this point and change it later), a running head, page header, page numbers, and byline/affiliation. You will be the only author listed here. The second page would just have the heading "Abstract." You do not need to write anything here yet. On the next page, you would list the title again. Because you don't have an Introduction written yet, we do not expect to see anything here, but if you have an idea of the key points you would like to make, go for it.

Following this, have the Methods header and subsections below that, followed by the Results, Discussion, and References headers. In the References section, we want to see the reference for your original study (at least). Be sure to use the APA format for this. Do not worry about figures and tables yet.

Feedback on these outlines will be returned to you in Lab #12, so that you can change incorrect formatting. Be sure to change your papers before submitting the next draft of your paper!

Final Note: Back up your work at all times! Do not save your paper in one place and run the risk of losing all of your work!

PSYCHOPHYSIOLOGICAL AND BEHAVIORAL (OBSERVATIONAL) PROCEDURES

Lab #12

Purpose:

- Learn about psychophysiological and behavioral (observational) research procedures.

Objectives:

- Review the following sections: Social Psychophysiological Research, Physiological Data, and Behavioral Observation Methods. Discuss the rationale for using psychophysiological and behavioral procedures.
- Learn about different types of research questions that can be answered with these procedures.
- Discuss various physiological measures (cardiac and vascular performance, facial electromyography, startle eye blink reflex responses, EMG activity, hormonal measures, etc.) and types of social phenomena they can index.
- Do in-class physiological demonstration and/or watch video clips demonstrating data collection using these methods.
- Discuss classification processes and benefits/limitations of systematic observation.
- Read and discuss Method section excerpts using psychophysiological and behavioral methods from published research articles.
- Operationalize hypothesis using psychophysiological and observational methods.

Homework:

- Complete behavioral observation exercise.
- Study for quiz on labs #11 and 12.

Social Psychophysiological Research

A GROWING number of social psychologists are taking advantage of relatively recent technological advances in order to answer their research questions. **Social psychophysiological methods** entail the manipulation of some social factor that elicits a psychological response, which is then measured via a carefully selected physiological indicator. For example, a researcher may be interested in how conflict between marital partners impacts how the partners' bodies recover from stress. To study this, couples might be asked to talk about a source of disagreement in their relationship over the course of an hour, during which time the researcher(s) will regularly collect saliva samples in order to measure their cortisol content (cortisol is a hormone produced when we experience stress).

There are a number of advantages to using psychophysiological methods. For example, many measures of emotion rely upon self-reports, in which participants indicate how they are feeling on a checklist, or they may be asked to rate their feelings on Likert-type scales. Physiological measures provide an indirect measure of our emotional experiences that is outside of participants' conscious control and, therefore, may be more objective. For example, a person assigned to interact with someone of a different racial group might say they felt comfortable during that interaction on a self-report survey; however, if they were hiding their true feelings, it is possible that their physiological responses could indicate otherwise (e.g., elevated heart rate and respiration rate).

There are a number of physiological responses that relate directly or indirectly to psychological experiences, including emotion, performance, stress, and personality. Let us consider a few examples. One way of assessing emotion is to measure muscle activity. Electromyography (EMG) is often used to measure electric potentials that are released when muscle fibers contract. For example, if electrodes are placed around the mouth and a participant contracts the *zygomaticus major* muscle (i.e., when that person smiles), we could infer that this person is experiencing happiness. In contrast, if the *currogator supercilii* muscle is activated (i.e., when that person frowns), we could infer that this person is experiencing sadness or displeasure. EMG is especially useful for detecting **microexpressions**, which are involuntary facial expressions that are expressed for just a fraction of a second. Some psychologists believe that microexpressions reflect concealed emotions (e.g., even when we are trying to hide something by controlling our words and body language, microexpressions may still "leak" out and reveal our true feelings; Ekman, Rolls, Perrett, & Ellis, 1992). Of course, having sensors attached to the face can be quite obtrusive to the participant. Hand movements are a potentially less cumbersome way to measure emotion, with greater pressure placed on the sensors indicating stronger emotion.

Sweat gland activation also occurs when people experience different types of emotions (e.g., arousal due to threat) and during cognitive activities. This type of activity is typically measured by galvanic skin response or electrodermal activity, which is typically most sensitive on the fingertips. Electrodes can be placed on participants' fingertips and changes in how a (non-painful) electric current is transmitted can demonstrate whether the sweat glands are activating in response to a stimulus.

Eye movements and pupillary responses are two other physiological responses to social stimuli. Pupillary response refers to dilation of the pupil, which is an indication of arousal or interest. Unfortunately, measuring pupil dilation can be challenging because any subtle changes in lighting can affect the measurement. Electro-oculography is used to assess eye movements (e.g., measuring rapid eye movements or REM during sleep). This technique is accomplished by placing electrodes around the eye. Beyond this, eye tracking technology has been developed to study what people pay attention to in particular contexts, such as what they look at in a room or what stimuli on a computer screen captures their attention first.

Measures of arousal frequently include cardiac and respiratory rate. Cardiac responses can be measured with electrocardiography, which measures electronic potentials of the heart muscle during each heartbeat. Increased heart rate is associated with greater arousal (e.g., feeling scared). Also, the variability of heart rate over time indicates how strongly one is experiencing an emotion, with increased levels indicating greater affect and decreased levels indicating a diminished experience. Respiration responses can reveal similar information. Researchers often examine both breathing rate and the exchange of oxygen and carbon dioxide. Bands can be placed around the lungs to measure rate and depth of respiration, and participants can inhale and exhale into sensors that detect how gases are exchanged.

Brain activation patterns are of interest to some psychophysiological researchers. For example, with electroencephalography (EEG), electrodes are placed around different points of the head to capture electronic activity, or neural firing in the brain. EEG has often been used to study stages of sleep (e.g., Stage 4 compared to REM sleep), but beyond that does not have much practical use for social psychologists. In contrast, functional magnetic resonance imaging (fMRI) is increasingly used by social psychologists because it can detect radiofrequency transmission within the brain. fMRI is much more sensitive than EEG in detecting changes in the firing of different neural connections.

Finally, biochemical measures entail capturing changes in hormonal, neurochemical, and even enzyme responses to stimuli. For example, serotonin and alpha amylase are both secreted (at different times) in response to threatening stimuli. Such responses are typically measured with saliva, or even blood, and analysis entails comparing levels of these chemicals and enzymes pre- and post-exposure to a stimulus. Many social psychologists use such measures to indicate arousal and response to threat, as well as to examine how long it takes people to recover from such exposure.

While psychophysiological data can help us to answer some really interesting research questions, it is not without its limitations. For one thing, such measures are typically very expensive and the results can be difficult to interpret. An hour of fMRI time for one participant can cost thousands of dollars, and even when you get your data, it may be difficult to discern whether autonomic arousal is really due to your experimental manipulation or to other factors. There are also many parameters to consider in the measurement of different physiological responses (e.g., wavelength, rates of firing), and some data collection systems may only allow certain parameters to be recorded. Also, the volume of data can be overwhelming to analyze, and computer systems need to be large enough to store and process such large data files. Ideally, researchers should triangulate, or use multiple methods to measure their dependent variables, such as using one or two different physiological measures in addition to self-report surveys.

References

Ekman, P., Rolls, E. T., Perrett, D. I., & Ellis, H. D. (1992). Facial expressions of emotion: An old controversy and new findings [and discussion]. *Philosophical Transactions of the Royal Society of London. Series B: Biological Sciences, 335*(1273), 63–69. doi: 10.1098/rstb.1992.0008

Physiological Data

Why Should You Consider Collecting It, and What Can It Tell You?

B ELOW is a chart outlining just a few physiological indicators that you may consider using, as well as some information on how to collect such data. Most physiological scanning equipment (e.g., Biopac, www.biopac.com) have instruments built into them to record basic indicators including heart rate and respiration, and other add-ons can be purchased to record additional indicators.

	What can it tell you?	Examples of equipment needed	How to do it
Heart rate/cardiac cycle	Autonomic nervous system activation	Photoplethysmograph	A small clip is placed on the finger, or measures taken with cuff at wrist, or other sites near arteries/veins
Respiration	Autonomic nervous system activation	Pneumatic belt	A thin belt is wrapped around the chest
Electrodermal (aka galvanic skin) response	Autonomic nervous system activation	Electrodes	Electrodes placed on index and middle finger
Eye tracking	Attention	Eye tracker devices, electrooculogram, or search coils	Eye-tracking setups vary greatly; some are head-mounted, some require the head to be stable (e.g., with a chin rest), and some function remotely and automatically track the head during motion.
Eye blinking	Startle response magnitude	Electromyogram (EMG)	Electrodes placed over the muscle beneath the lower eyelid)
Brain activity	Brain activation patterns	Electroencephalography (EEG) Functional magnetic resonance imaging (fMRI) Positron emission tomography (PET)	EEG: electrodes placed on head fMRI: Participant placed in an MRI scanner PET: Participant placed in a PET scanner

Vocal characteristics	Arousal level	Microphone and voice program software (e.g., Multidimensional Voice Program software program by KayPentax; Lincoln Park, NJ)	Participant is recorded, and vocal amplitude, pitch, tone, and other vocal indicators can be analyzed
Facial behaviors	Valence of emotion	Electromyogram (EMG) Observation (e.g., Facial Action Coding System, Ekman & Friesen, 1978)	Electrodes placed over muscle groups between the eyebrows and corner of the lips
Whole-body behaviors	Numerous things (e.g., emotions, level of arousal, feelings of comfort or discomfort)	Observation	Participant can be directly observed, or their behaviors can be recorded and coded
Testosterone	Response to threat or erotic stimuli	Saliva collection or blood serum	Participants provide saliva samples, or blood draws can be taken
Alpha-amylase	Response to threat and stress	Saliva collection	Participants provide saliva samples

Note:

Autonomic nervous system (ANS) activation: This can indicate emotional responding (e.g., fear, anger, sadness), arousal states, and basic physiological functions, such as digestion. Important note: Not all of the ANS responses can map onto a single dimension (e.g., anger), so it is sometimes hard to understand exactly what this data is telling you.

Startle response magnitude: This describes a universal reflexive response that serves a protective function when things are perceived as potentially threatening. It can help assess whether—and how—threatening stimuli are to the perceiver (reactivity).

Brain activation patterns: Measures of brain activity (i.e., EEG) often contrast activation across different segments of the brain (e.g., left and right hemispheres), and can be an indication of emotion and approach/avoidance responses. Greater signal detection in certain parts of the brain shows that stimuli are activating those particular regions, and that information is being processed there.

Whole-body behaviors: Many things can be examined here. For example, a person's posture can demonstrate emotions such as pride and sadness; the distance one person sits from someone else can indicate comfort level; the total amount of movement can reveal how emotionally aroused one is; etc.

The next pages are excerpts from two research articles using psychophysiological or observational methods. You will read through these during class time and discuss.

The Psychophysiology of James Bond

Phasic Emotional Responses to Violent Video Game Events

By Niklas Ravaja, Marko Turpeinen, Timo Saari, Sampsa Puttonen, and Liisa Keltikangas-Järvinen

Method

Participants

PARTICIPANTS were 36 Finnish undergraduate students (25 men and 11 women; age range = 20–30 years). All participants played video or computer games at least once a month. They participated in return for three movie tickets.

Video Games

We used two video games: "James Bond 007: NightFire" (Electronic Arts Inc., Redwood City, CA) and "Super Monkey Ball 2" (Sega Corporation, Tokyo; nonviolent control condition). The games were played with the Nintendo GameCube (Nintendo Co., Ltd., Kyoto, Japan) and were presented on a screen using the Panasonic PT-LC75E Multimedia Projector. The image size was 114 cm (width) X 85 cm (height), and the distance between the player's eyes and the screen was about 200 cm.

"James Bond 007: NightFire." In this game, the player acts as James Bond, a secret agent, and has to use different weapons (e.g., pistol, rifle, assault rifle) and spy craft gadgetry. As Bond, the player operates in the snow-capped French Alps to defeat the criminal mastermind Rafael Drake. The practice session was played at the "operative"

difficulty level, and the two actual game sessions, easy and difficult, were played at the "agent" and "00 agent" difficulty levels, respectively. The game is played from the first-person view and contains realistic graphics. When the player's character wounds an opponent, the opponent cries out with pain and his body movements indicate that he was hit. When the player's character kills an opponent, the opponent cries out with pain and falls down. When the player's character is wounded, the (first-person) view pulsates with reddish light for a while, the player receives haptic feedback (control paddle vibrates), and an indicator in the corner of the game screen shows a reduction in the vitality of the player's character. When the player's character is fatally hit, the player receives haptic feedback (control paddle vibrates), all actions are disabled, and transparent (red) blood begins to flow down from the top of the player's view (game screen) eventually tingeing the whole view red (this takes about 6 s).

"Super Monkey Ball 2." The game takes place in a surrealistic world with bright colors and includes a game board hanging in the air and a cute little monkey (i.e., player's character) trapped in a transparent ball. The player's task is to tilt the board to roll the ball toward a particular goal without falling off the edge of the board into the depths. The player needs to avoid obstacles and pick objects (e.g., bananas) as the monkey rolls around the stages.

Procedure

After a brief description of the experiment, each participant gave their written informed consent. Electrodes were then attached, and the participant was seated in a comfortable armchair in a dimly illuminated room, followed by a rest period of 7 min. The participants played four different video games in random order. There were three 5-min game sessions for each of the four games: a practice session and two actual play sessions (i.e., easy and difficult). In the present study, we used only data from "James Bond 007: NightFire" and "Super Monkey Ball 2." The participant was told that the three best male and female gamers would be awarded one movie ticket as a bonus.

Measures

Mood during game playing. We defined mood in terms of the following five affective feeling states: joy, pleasant relaxation, fear, anger, and depressed feeling. We constructed two- or three-item scales consisting of affect terms to assess the affective feeling states (see Ravaja, 2004b; Watson, Wiese, Vaidya, & Tellegen, 1999). Specifically, the items were as follows: joyful, lively, and enthusiastic (joy); relaxed and calm (pleasant relaxation); fearful and nervous (fear); angry, annoyed, and aggressive (anger); and depressed, tired, and dull (depression). The participants were asked to indicate the extent to which they felt this way during the preceding game. Each item was rated on a 7-point scale ranging from 1 (not at all) to 7 (extremely much).

Psychoticism. Psychoticism as a personality trait was measured with the Psychoticism scale of the Eysenck Personality Questionnaire—Revised, Short Form (S. B. G. Eysenck, Eysenck, & Barrett, 1985). The Psychoticism scale includes 12 items (e.g., "Would you like other people to be afraid of you?" and "Do you try not to be rude to people?" [reverse scored]) that require a yes–no response (Cronbach's a = .65). On the basis of a median split of the total Psychoticism score (separately by gender), participants were identified as belonging to either a high-psychoticism group or a low-psychoticism group.

Physiological Data Collection

Facial EMG activity was recorded from the left corrugator supercilii, zygomaticus major, and orbicularis oculi muscle regions, as recommended by Fridlund and Cacioppo (1986), using surface silver/silver chloride (Ag/AgCl) electrodes with a contact area of 4 mm diameter (Med Associates Inc., St. Albans, VT). Electrodes were filled with TD-240 electrode gel (Med Associates Inc). The raw EMG signal was amplified, and frequencies below 30 Hz and above 400 Hz were filtered out using the Psylab Model EEG8 amplifier (Contact Precision Instruments, Boston). The raw signal was rectified and integrated using the Psylab INT8 contour (Contact Precision Instruments) following integrator (time constant = 50 ms).

Skin conductance level (SCL) was recorded with the Psylab Model SC5 24 bit digital skin conductance amplifier (Contact Precision Instruments), which applied a constant 0.5 V across Ag/AgCl electrodes with a contact area of 8 mm diameter (Med Associates Inc.). Electrodes were filled with TD-246 skin conductance electrode paste (Med Associates Inc.) and attached to the middle phalanges of the ring and little fingers of each participant's nondominant hand after hands were washed with soap and water.

The digital data collection was controlled by Psylab7 (Contact Precision Instruments) software, and all physiological signals were sampled at a rate of 500 Hz.

Video Recording of the Game

During the game, the output signal (video and audio) from the GameCube was stored as digital video (25 frames/s) with the V1d Random

Access Video Recorder/Player (Doremi Labs, Inc., Burbank, CA). The recorded video image of the game screen was in time synchrony with the physiological data with a one-frame (40-ms) accuracy.

Event Scoring

The exact onset times of predefined game events were determined by examining the played games, frame by frame, using V-ToolsPro 2.20 software (Doremi Labs, Inc.). We scored the following game events from "James Bond 007: NightFire": (a) The player's character (James Bond) wounded an opponent with a gun (Opponent Wounded event, mean $f = 20.8$, range = 5–38), (b) the player's character killed an opponent with a gun (Opponent Killed event, mean $f = 16.1$, range = 3–27), (c) the player's character was wounded from gunfire (Bond Wounded event, mean $f = 27.0$, range = 7–73), and (d) the player's character was killed by an opponent's gunfire (Bond Killed event, mean $f = 1.8$, range = 0–8). One nonviolent game event was scored from "Super Monkey Ball 2": The monkey picks a banana (and the player earns points; Picking a Banana event, mean $f = 24.1$, range = 7–52). None of the events was systematically preceded or followed by other events.

Data Reduction and Analysis

Mean values for the psychophysiological measures were derived for one 1-s epoch before each event (Second 1) and for six 1-s epochs after event onset (Seconds 2–7). Logarithmic transformations were conducted for physiological data to normalize the distributions. The data were analyzed by the linear mixed-models procedure in SPSS with restricted maximum likelihood estimation and a first-order autoregressive covariance structure for the residuals. When examining the main effects of game events, the difficulty level, sequence number of an event, and second were selected as factors, and a fixed-effects model that included

the main effects of these variables was specified. When comparing the responses elicited by violent and nonviolent events, (type of) event was also selected as a factor, and the main effect of event and the Event X Second interaction were added to the fixed-effects model. Furthermore, when examining the interactive effects of psychoticism and game events on physiological activity, the dichotomized Psychoticism score, difficulty level, sequence number of an event, and second were selected as factors, and a fixed-effects model that included the main effects of these variables and the Psychoti- cism X Second interaction was specified.

Event-related changes in physiological activity were tested using the following contrasts: (a) Second 1 versus Seconds 2 to 7 (Contrast 1), (b) Picking a Banana versus Opponent Wounded X Second 1 versus Seconds 2 to 7 (Contrast 2), (c) Picking a Banana versus Opponent Killed X Second 1 versus Seconds 2 to 7 (Contrast 3), and (d) Low Psychoticism versus High Psychoticism X Second 1 versus Seconds 2 to 7 (Contrast 4). In some cases, physiological responses were of a relatively short duration and not captured by Contrast 1. In these cases, post hoc contrasts based on visual inspection of the response curves were used.

Social Support in Couples

An Examination of Gender Differences Using Self-Report and Observational Methods

By Lesley L. Verhofstadt, Ann Buysse, and William Ickes

Study 2: Method

Participants

THE sample consisted of the 64 members of 32 Belgian married couples. Advertisements were placed in magazines and newspapers recruiting couples who were willing to participate in a research project on close relationships. The couples who responded positively to the recruitment ads were given a standard description of the project and were evaluated for their eligibility to participate. To participate, the members of each couple had to have been involved in their heterosexual relationship for at least 1 year, and to have been married for at least 6 months. The eligible couples who expressed interest in participating in the study were scheduled to attend a laboratory session. They were told that the study concerned close relationships, and that they would be asked to complete some questionnaires.

The demographic characteristics of the participants are reported in Table 1. In the present study, men and women reported a mean marital quality score of 116.00 (SD =11.71, range=96-134) and 114.81 (SD=10.86, range=98-139), respectively, on the Dyadic Adjustment Scale (DAS; Spanier 1976). Dyadic Adjustment Scale norms report a mean marital quality score of 114/115 for a married sample, thereby indicating that our sample is comparable to an average group of married couples in terms of marital quality.

Procedure

After providing their informed consent, the participants completed a set of questionnaires, including the SSIQ and the QRI.

Interaction Session

The participants were led into a laboratory that was furnished as a living room, and was equipped so that the couple's interaction could be videotaped with their prior knowledge. Following the procedure used in previous observational research on social support in marriage, the spouses were asked to discuss a salient personal problem that was formally designated as being either the man's or the woman's problem. To ensure sufficient variability, the gender of the support seeker (man vs. woman) was systematically counterbalanced (see also Verhofstadt et al. 2005a). When both partners had agreed to discuss the issue, they were instructed to try to act much as they would at home when discussing an important personal problem with each other. The partners were allowed to interact as long as they considered necessary, up to a maximum time limit of 30 min.

Lesley L. Verhofstadt, Ann Buysse, and William Ickes, "Social Support in Couples: An Examination of Gender Differences Using Self-Report and Observational Methods," *Sex Roles*, vol. 57, no. 3–4, pp. 274–275. Copyright © 2007 by Springer Science+Business Media. Reprinted with permission.

Video Review Procedure

Immediately after their interaction had been recorded, the partners were seated separately and asked to complete a video-review task (e.g., Fletcher and Thomas 2000; Sillars et al. 2000; Verhofstadt et al. 2005b). The partners were asked to imagine living through and re-experiencing their interaction again while they each viewed a videotaped copy of the interaction. Every 60 s, the videotape paused automatically and the participants were instructed to report their on-line perception of being supported by their partner at that specific point of time in the interaction. This computerized procedure served the purpose of selecting several random time samples (M= 17) from the interaction during which some form of spousal support was presumably given and received, and how the support process was experienced by each spouse in the interaction.

The average internal consistency for this on-line support perception index across the several time samples was .86 for husbands and .90 for wives. These high alpha values justified our decision to aggregate the on-line perception scores for the various time samples into a global index for on-line perceived support during the interaction (see De Clercq et al. 2001). This score reflected the participants' experience of being supported during the interaction. At the end of the session, the members of each couple were fully debriefed.

Measures

Support Behaviors

See Study 1 for a description of this measure. The Cronbach's alphas ranged between .68 and .94 for the husbands, and between .68 and .93 for the wives.

Perceived Support

See Study 1 for a description of this measure. Cronbach's alpha was .80 for the husbands and .82 for the wives.

Observed Support Behaviors

The behavioral data were analyzed with a rating system based on the Social Support Interaction Coding System (SSICS, Bradbury and Pasch 1994), which was specifically developed for studying the support solicitation and provision behavior of partners during discussions of personal, non-marital difficulties. Five SSICS categories were used for this study: (a) Positive Helpee Behavior (e.g., gives clear analysis of problem, recognizes partner as an aid, agrees with suggestions of helper, expresses feelings related to the problem); (b) Negative Helpee Behavior (e.g., rejects help, criticizes helper, makes demands for support, whines or complains); (c) Positive Emotional Helper Behavior (e.g., reassures, encourages expression of feelings, provides genuine encouragement); (d) Positive Instrumental Helper Behavior (e.g., offers specific plan or assistance, gives helpful advice, asks specific questions aimed at defining the problem); and (e) Negative Helper Behavior (e.g., criticizes, minimizes problem, is inattentive or disengaged, offers unhelpful advice). Each behavioral category was rated on a 7-point scale ranging from not at all (1) to very much (7).

Three undergraduate observers participated in a rater training in which they memorized the description of SSICS categories, and then practice coded a set of pilot tapes. They then compared their scoring and discussed their rating problems with each other. With respect to each of the interactions included in the data for the present study, they were told only who the support seeker (man vs. woman) was and were kept "blind" with respect to all of the other variables being studied.

The three trained observers first viewed the entire videotaped interaction before rating it to obtain an overview of the support interaction. The observers then viewed the interaction again and separately rated the behavior of each partner in each interaction, alternating between the husbands' and wives' behavior. During the actual rating process, a computer program paused the videotape after each 60 s (i.e., at exactly the same moments in the interaction as during the video-review task). Our trained observers then used the behavioral cues that occurred during these 60-s time samples to rate the partners' behaviors. Thirty percent of the interactions were rated by three observers, and the levels of interobserver agreement were calculated with Cronbach's alpha for each of the behaviors that were rated. The alpha values we obtained ranged from .74 to .93. All of the interobserver alphas indicated good levels of interobserver reliability.

On-line Perceived Support

On-line perceived support was assessed by means of a 7-point rating scale (1 = not at all, and 7 = very much) on which the partners indicated the extent to which they felt helped and supported during the interaction.

Behavioral Observation Methods

LIKE psychophysiological research methods, behavioral observation is another way that social psychologists can get around some of the limitations of self-report data. Behavioral observation is fairly straightforward. After you have a research question, you identify your sample and then select the set of behaviors that would serve as your dependent variable(s). There are any number of characteristics related to your chosen behavior that might be of interest, such as the frequency, magnitude (intensity), and duration of time that the behavior is exhibited.

If you conduct a study using behavioral observation, your research question needs to be extremely specific. For example, if your research question concerns whether men are more aggressive than women, this would likely be far too ambiguous. What is meant by "aggressive?" Are you referring to verbal aggression (e.g., yelling)? Physical aggression (e.g., slapping or hitting)? Also, what contexts are you considering? Is provocation necessary? Does the participant need to be frustrated? You need to know which specific behaviors illustrate the type of aggression you are after and determine how feasible it will be to observe such behaviors in your study.

Observational research can be conducted in manipulated or non-manipulated environments. Non-manipulated means that you simply conduct a naturalistic observation, such as observing a set of behaviors at a local playground or at a restaurant. This type of study has the advantage of being non-obtrusive (most participants may not know that they are being observed and therefore act naturally); however, it is correlational, meaning that it is impossible to make inferences about cause and effect. There is no true control group in a naturalistic observation and there could be numerous factors in the environment that are contributing to the observed behavior of which the researcher may not be fully aware. In contrast, manipulated environments refer to experimental or quasi-experimental designs in which the experimenter alters some aspect of the research environment and observes what happens. For example, the researcher might have participants sit in a room and collaborate with another participant on a difficult task while the temperature in the room slowly increases to an uncomfortable level. The control group would complete the same task but experience no such temperature increase. The researcher would then observe what happens and code aggressive behaviors that occur in those different temperature environments.

Observational methods can be used in the lab or in field settings, and both can be either manipulated or non-manipulated environments. The observations can be coded by observers as behaviors unfold, but typically behaviors are recorded with video or audio and coded at a later point in time when the researchers can more carefully review the record and make corrections to their data if needed. **Inter-rater reliability** is very important in this type of research, meaning that you want to be sure that all of your coders are well-trained and are coding observations the same way. For example, while the coding protocol may explicitly state that aggressive behavior may include slapping, how should an attempted slap be coded? In other words, if a person were to raise their hand and threaten to slap someone, would that count as an act of aggression? Such nuances in coding behaviors make it essential to have multiple coders who are able to discuss areas of disagreement and resolve what specific behaviors mean in relation to the research question. All of this helps to ensure greater objectivity.

While the objectivity and non-obtrusiveness of (some) behavioral observational research is a major strength of this method, it is not without its weaknesses. Some behaviors are difficult or impossible to observe, such as private sexual activity and cognitive processes. Therefore, this method cannot answer all research questions. In addition, there is always the possibility that participants may realize that they are being observed, which may make them upset or cause them to act unnaturally. Researchers must plan for how they will handle possible discovery if they are conducting naturalistic observations, because informed consent and debriefing are typically not possible in such situations.

Operationalization of Hypothesis: Physiological or Observational Methods

COMPLETE the following exercise in your group during the lab. You will present your answers in front of the class, and then have a discussion. Afterward, submit the form to your lab instructor.

Names of individuals in your group:

1. Original hypothesis:

2. If you were to use a physiological or observational method for your study, how would you operationalize your hypothesis? Has this method ever been used to test hypotheses similar to yours? How? To what effect?

3. What are some possible benefits of using this method to test your hypothesis?

4. What are some possible limitations of using this method to test your hypothesis?

5. What ethical issues (if any) might you have if you used a physiological or observational method to test your hypothesis? How might you overcome these issues? (*Hint: Have any other studies had to address these issues?*)

Behavioral Observation Exercise

For this assignment, you are to pair up with another person in your lab group for a field observation exercise. You will have to visit a coffee shop, bar, cafeteria, or restaurant together and observe four three-minute interactions between two people. In lab groups of four, two people should observe same-sex dyads, and two should observe different-sex dyads. If you are in a lab group of two to three people, you should select either four same-sex or different-sex dyads to code.

When you are in your field setting, you and your partner(s) should place yourselves such that you can easily view and hear your dyad, but not conspicuously. You will observe their behaviors as unobtrusively as possible. One of you should keep track of time, because you will only be observing their behaviors for three minutes. After each minute passes, signal each other to be sure to record behavioral frequency, one minute at a time.

Using the behavioral coding sheet that follows, you will indicate the frequency of smiling, laughing, and joking in your targeted dyad. Then, you will rate the dyad on a set of 5-point Likert scale measures. After you have assessed your dyads, answer the questions on the summary sheet. You will turn all of these sheets in to your lab instructor at the next lab meeting

Behavioral Coding Sheet

Dyad #1

Describe Person A:_____

Describe Person B:_____

Tally behaviors for each person over a three-minute period.

Indicator	Minute 1		Minute 2	
	A	B	A	B
Smile				
Joke				
Laugh				

Indicator	Minute 3		Total (add across all minutes)	
	A	B	A	B
Smile				
Joke				
Laugh				

How friendly would you rate person A?

1	2	3	4	5
Not friendly at all		Neutral		Very friendly

How friendly would you rate person B?

1	2	3	4	5
Not friendly at all		Neutral		Very friendly

Behavioral Coding Sheet

Dyad #2

Describe Person A:_____

Describe Person B:_____

Tally behaviors for each person over a three-minute period.

	Minute 1		Minute 2	
	A	B	A	B
Smile				
Joke				
Laugh				

	Minute 3		Total (add across all minutes)	
	A	B	A	B
Smile				
Joke				
Laugh				

How friendly would you rate person A?

1	2	3	4	5
Not friendly at all		Neutral		Very friendly

How friendly would you rate person B?

1	2	3	4	5
Not friendly at all		Neutral		Very friendly

Behavioral Coding Sheet

Dyad #3

Describe Person A:_____

Describe Person B:_____

Tally behaviors for each person over a three-minute period.

	Minute 1		Minute 2	
	A	B	A	B
Smile				
Joke				
Laugh				

	Minute 3		Total (add across all minutes)	
	A	B	A	B
Smile				
Joke				
Laugh				

How friendly would you rate person A?

1	2	3	4	5
Not friendly at all		Neutral		Very friendly

How friendly would you rate person B?

1	2	3	4	5
Not friendly at all		Neutral		Very friendly

Behavioral Coding Sheet

Dyad #4

Describe Person A:_____

Describe Person B:_____

Tally behaviors for each person over a three-minute period.

	Minute 1		Minute 2	
	A	B	A	B
Smile				
Joke				
Laugh				

	Minute 3		Total (add across all minutes)	
	A	B	A	B
Smile				
Joke				
Laugh				

How friendly would you rate person A?

1	2	3	4	5
Not friendly at all		Neutral		Very friendly

How friendly would you rate person B?

1	2	3	4	5
Not friendly at all		Neutral		Very friendly

Behavioral Observation Exercise Summary Sheet

1. In what setting did you complete your behavioral observation?

2. What time of day and what day of the week did you complete this exercise?

3. Did you observe same-sex or different-sex dyads?

4. How similar were your behavioral ratings to those of your partner(s)? What do you think accounts for any discrepancies that you may have had?

5. After comparing your coding sheets with your partner(s), did you notice any significant differences between dyadic partners in their smiling, joking, or laughing behaviors? What do you think accounts for those differences, if there were any at all? If there were no differences that you could see, why would this be so?

6. What influence, if any, do you think your field location, time of day, and day of week had on your behavioral sampling?

7. Do you think that you would have found any differences between the dyad type that you coded and the other type that you did not code (same-sex versus different-sex dyads)? What would you anticipate those differences to be? Why?

8. If you could go back and redo your behavioral coding with your partner(s), what would you do differently?

SMALL GROUP RESEARCH PROCEDURES

Lab #13

Purpose:

- Learn about small group research procedures.

Objectives:

- Quiz for labs #11 and 12.
- Discuss behavioral coding exercise in class.
- Review the following section entitled Small Group Research Procedures and discuss the rationale for utilizing this method in social psychological research.
- Learn about different types of research questions that can be answered with this procedure.
- Learn about strategies for small group research (field and archival research, observational field methods, field experiments, lab experiments, systematic observation).
- Read and discuss Method section excerpts using small group methods from published research articles.
- Operationalize hypothesis using small group research.
- Learn about analysis issues with group research.

Homework:

- Submit a draft of the Introduction to your paper.

Small Group Research Procedures

Given that social psychologists are interested in how our social environments impact our thoughts, feelings and behaviors, it should be no surprise that some research questions are best answered by studying people in group contexts. Conflict communication, helping behaviors, creativity, and decision-making processes are among the many types of behaviors that can be studied in such settings. Depending upon the outcome of interest, small group procedures can yield quantitative (e.g., total number of ideas produced) or qualitative data (e.g., the content of the ideas produced). Additionally, such studies can be conducted in-person (all the group together at one time) or virtually (e.g., Internet chat sessions), depending upon the researchers' needs.

Groups are defined as two or more people, which means that research in this area can include everyone from romantic couples, roommates, and friends, to large work groups and classrooms. The type of group you study depends on your research question. If you are interested in intimate relationships, you might recruit married couples or families for your study. If you are interested in testing different methods of producing group cohesion among strangers, then you might simply recruit groups of 4-6 people to attend your experiment at a specific time. Regardless of the type of group you select, small group research can demonstrate what people actually do in a group context, which is far more valuable than asking people how they think they might act in the presence of others.

The type of data you can collect in small group research also depends upon your research question. For example, you could video record interactions of groups and then conduct a behavioral observation analysis (described earlier in this book). Alternatively, you might survey each participant in the group separately, and have them rate each other on a number of variables (e.g., likeability, relative power). You could also audio record the conversations that your groups have and then conduct a qualitative analysis of the general themes that emerge. The sky is the limit in terms of how you decide to measure your variables. The only real difference between this type of research and the others covered in this manual so far is that there are multiple people in the study at the same time rather than just one.

Small group research has a number of strengths. One important strength is that this method allows researchers to obtain information about interpersonal interactions rather than just examining one person in isolation. Another strength is that, oftentimes, small group work is more engrossing and engaging than the tasks employed in a typical study, which means that participants sometimes "forget" or are not focused on the fact that they are in a psychological research study. These absorbing or engrossing tasks (e.g., role playing, discussing an issue) can therefore produce **mundane realism** and resemble what a participant may do in real life.

Of course, such research has its limitations. For example, it may be challenging to recruit and schedule all group members needed for your study. And even if you do get everyone to commit to a certain date and time, some group members may fail to show up. Such challenges make this form of research very difficult and time-consuming to execute. Another limitation is that the nature of the group interactions can make data analyses complicated. Consider that even when people interact in groups of strangers, norms and intergroup dynamics develop over time, which leads participants within a given group to respond to each other in a unique way that is very different from other groups. For example, after completing a task in a group setting, participants may start to like or dislike each other, and those feelings may affect how participants respond for the duration of the study. For groups that existed prior to a study (e.g., married couples, families), this issue is even more pronounced, because group members are interdependent and have longstanding roles that they play in their group and certain norms that they adhere to. This means that each person in a small group study is not "independent." This is problematic because independence is an assumption of many statistical approaches used to analyze data (e.g., analysis of variance and regression). Therefore, when analyzing small group data, researchers must account for the fact that data within groups are correlated with each other, and this can make such statistical analyses complex.

The next pages are excerpts from two research articles using small group research methods. You will read through these during class time and discuss.

Autocracy Bias in Informal Groups Under Need for Closure

By Antonio Pierro, Lucia Mannetti, Eraldo De Grada, Stefano Livi, and Arie W. Kruglanski

Overview and Design

PARTICIPANTS in 12 leaderless groups of four members each role-played the managers of four corporate departments meeting to negotiate the division of a monetary prize among four candidates representing their respective sectors. To that end, each manager was provided with his or her own candidate's resume. Six groups were composed of individuals with high dispositional need for closure and the remaining six of individuals dispositionally low on this need. The main dependent measures included (a) two asymmetry indices computed for each group (respectively referring to obtained and maintained turns) and (b) ratings of each member's interactional style scored for the degree of autocracy.

Dispositional Need for Closure

One to 2 months prior to the experimental session, participants in large groups filled out a battery of various instruments including the Italian version of the Need for Closure Scale (De Grada, Kruglanski, Mannetti, Pierro, & Webster, 1996; Mannetti, Pierro, Kruglanski, Taris, & Bezinovic, 2002; Pierro et al., 1995; Webster & Kruglanski, 1994).

As originally developed by Webster and Kruglanski (1994), this scale includes five subscales respectively related to (a) need for order, (b) intolerance of ambiguity, (c) closed-mindedness, (d) need for predictability, and (e) decisiveness. Recent research using the Italian and the American versions of the scale (De Grada et al., 1996; Kruglanski et al., 1997; Mannetti et al., 2002; Pierro et al., 1995) has indicated that even though the structural analyses of the Need for Closure (NFC) scale are compatible with either a one or a two (second-order) independent-factor solution, the decisiveness subscale exhibits inconsistent relations with the remaining subscales and occasionally relates differently to external constructs (for discussions of the psychometric properties of the scale, see Kruglanski et al., 1997; Mannetti etal., 2002; Neuberg, Judice, & West, 1997). For this reason, in the present study we used a reduced version of the NFC scale without the decisiveness items.

To assess the structure of such a reduced Need for Closure Scale, a confirmatory factor analysis was conducted by means of Lisrel VIII (Joreskog & Sorbom, 1993). Specifically, the one-factor model was tested and confronted with the null model. It was found that the one-factor model, $\%^2(\text{df} = 2) = 2.00$, p = .37, fits the data better than the null model, $\%^2(\text{df} = 6) = 49.11$, p = .001, and has a very good comparative fit index (CFI = 1.00) (Bentler, 1990). All of the facets showed significant factor loadings ranging from .77 for fear of ambiguity to .71 for need for predictability to .67 for need for order and .55

for close-mindedness. Therefore, in this study the scores of the four subscales were summed up to a reliable total score of Need for Closure (Cronbach's a = .89). Individuals scoring above the median of the scale were classified as high, and those below the median were classified as low on the need for closure.

Participants agreed to participate in simulated group discussions and were, therefore, invited to appear in the social psychological laboratory. Twenty-four participants high in the need for closure were randomly assigned to six groups comprising the high need for closure condition; similarly, 24 participants low in the need for closure were randomly assigned to six groups comprising the low need for closure condition. To demonstrate that the resulting two categories of groups effectively differed from each other on the need for closure, a one-way ANOVA was performed on the Need for Closure scores. As expected, the difference between the low (M = 112.21) and the high (M = 137.42) NFC groups was highly significant, $F(1, 10) = 19.46$, $p < .001$.

Procedure

Participants volunteered for a study concerned with a simulation of a group discussion. They were scheduled to appear at an appointed time at the Department of Social and Developmental Psychology at the University of Rome. After arriving, participants were greeted by an experimenter (A.P.) who ushered them to a room and seated them around a table. The experimenter then delivered the instructions designed to introduce to participants the group task they were about to perform.

Specifically, each participant was asked to role-play a department manager at a meeting of an Awards Committee of their (American) corporation. These managers were described as, respectively, the heads of the sales, marketing, data-processing, and social-benefits departments. The committee's task was to consider four subordinates nominated for a merit-based monetary

award in accordance with the company's policy of rewarding its workers for special achievements. Each participant was further told that the company's limited resources did not allow it to make a substantial award to all the deserving candidates. For the specific year under consideration (1980), only $5,000 in award funds were available for distribution.

Participants were further told that the four candidates (e.g., Roger Smith from the Sales Department) all came from departments whose heads were members of the Awards Committee. Information about each candidate included a brief resume and a recommendation letter from the candidate's supervisor justifying his or her nomination for the award. Each participant also was told to imagine that he or she had already discussed the candidate with his or her supervisor who convinced him or her of his or her ample deservingness for the award.

During the committee's discussion, each participant's task was (a) to present valid arguments in favor of her or his candidate and (b) to help the committee to arrive at a best decision as to the allocation of the available funds. The "committee members" (i.e., the participants) were instructed to state their recommendation in a common written document. Failure to reach a joint decision was to result in a cancellation of all awards for that year. After they had received these instructions, the four participants commenced their negotiations.

The group discussions lasted 56 min on the average. Unbeknownst to the participants, the experimental room where the group deliberations took place contained a one-way mirror concealing a video camera that recorded the entire group interaction. Participants learned this at the end of the group discussion and were asked their permission to allow the use of the video recordings for research purposes. All participants complied with this request.

After completion of the entire study, participants were thoroughly debriefed and the purpose of the study was fully explained to them. This concluded the experiment.

Measuring the Dependent Variables

Floor control. The group discussions were transcribed following the notational system routinely employed in conversational analysis, developed originally by Gail Jefferson (1985; for a thorough description of the system and its development see Psathas & Anderson, 1990). Judges blind to the need for closure condition used each group's transcript to calculate two indices of conversational floor control: the number of speaking turns successfully seized by each member (i.e., turns obtained) and the number of such turns successfully maintained despite interruption attempts by others. Each member's floor gain index was then computed by dividing the total number of his or her obtained turns by the total number of obtained turns for the entire group. Similarly, the member's floor defense index was calculated by dividing his or her total number of maintained turns by the total number of maintained turns for the entire group.

For each group, we then computed the following two indices: (a) its asymmetry of floor gain index operationally defined as the ratio of the standard deviation to the mean of members' floor gain scores and (b) its asymmetry of floor defense index operationally defined as the ratio of the standard deviation to the mean of members' floor defense scores. The logic of these indices is as follows: The standard deviation in each group reflects asymmetry or variability in the degree to which group members control the floor in terms of obtained and maintained turns. But the different groups may vary also in the overall intensity with which their members attempted to control the floor. To standardize these indices, we divided the standard deviations of each group by the mean of members' floor gain or floor defense scores for that group. The resulting measure is known statisti-callyasthe "coefficient of variation" (cf. Armitage, 1971; Vogt, 1993) and is

commonly used to compare standard deviations derived from different distributions.

Members' autocratic style. Two independent observers used a 5-point scale to rate each member on the following four dimensions: authoritarianism, dogmatism, assertiveness, and egocentrism. Each participant was assigned the average of the two observers' ratings. To assess the observers' reliability, we followed Rosenthal's (1987, pp. 9–13) suggestion by correlating the two sets of counts and using the Spearman-Brown prophecy formula to derive the final reliability index (see also McLeod, Baron, Marti, & Yoon, 1997; Stasser & Stewart, 1992; Stewart & Stasser, 1996). The interrater agreement for the four scales was .80 for authoritarianism, .52 for dogmatism, .76 for assertiveness, and .78 for egocentrism. A principal components analysis was applied to the four items. On the first factor that explained 74% of the total variance, all of the items manifested high loadings (.58 for assertiveness, .97 for authoritarianism, .90 for egocentrism, and .93 for dogmatism). Cronbach's alpha for the total scale was .87, and the interrater agreement for the total scale was .84.

Members' influence over the group process. Our theory assumes that members who dominate the discussion and exert a high degree of floor control exert also a proportionate degree of influence on the remaining members. We used two separate measures of members' influence: (a) independent observer ratings and (b) each member's rank ordering of all four members (including themselves) in regard to the degree to which he or she influenced the final decision. With respect to the first measure, two independent observers rated each member using a 5-point scale on two items: (a) the extent to which the member was dominant during the group process and (b) the extent to which he or she was submissive. To assess the observers' reliability, we again followed Rosenthal's (1987, pp. 9–13) suggestion by correlating the two sets of counts and using the Spearman-Brown prophecy formula to derive the final reliability index (see also McLeod et al., 1997; Stasser & Stewart, 1992; Stewart & Stasser, 1996). The interrater agreement for the two scales was, respectively, .73 for dominance and .77 for submission. After reversing the submission item, the correlation between the two items was .94 and the interrater agreement for the entire scale was .79.

With regard to the second measure, we used the mean of the ranks assigned each participant by the four group members as an index of her or his influence. For ease of exposition, we appropriately inverted the rank score so that the higher numbers indicated the greater perceived influence.

Nominal Group Technique, Social Loafing, and Group Creative Project Quality

By Cheryl L. Asmus and Keith James

Study 1

USE of the NGT and prior awareness of individual evaluation were both expected to encourage individual effort (reduce loafing) and, through this mechanism, to improve the quality of the performance of the groups in those conditions. In other words, main effects of both NGT and of salient individual evaluation were hypothesized with both of those effects mediated by impacts on social loafing.

Method

The NGT was used by students in some project groups in some laboratory sections of a class and not used by other groups in the other laboratory sections of the same class. In addition, a method for grading group projects that included evaluation of individual contributions was developed and used to grade the group projects. Members of some project groups were told before they engaged in work on the project that individual contributions would be formally evaluated by other group members; members of other groups were not informed about the peer-evaluation of individual contributions until after the project work was done. Projects required both generation of a creative idea and planning of how to effectively execute the idea.

Project groups were from four separate sections of the social psychology laboratory in the same

semester. There were 16 students in each section for a total of 64 participants across all sections. Students were randomly assigned to four-person groups (yielding a total of 16 project groups) to work on developing new research ideas on a defined topic. Each group had to not only generate a research idea but also had to work out written and oral presentations of that idea. Because the most common definition of creativity is something that is novel and useful (Amabile, 1996), the group projects here that involved generating new (novel) research ideas and using them as the core of a presentation for course credit qualified as substantially creative.

In two of the sections (randomly selected), groups were simply given their assignment and left on their own to plan and execute it. In the other two sections, groups were instructed on the two-stages of NGT and told to follow them in completing each element (idea generation, planning of written and oral presentations) of the group project. In one of the two NGT sections (randomly selected) and one of the non-NGT sections (randomly selected), the four project groups were given (orally and in writing) an explanation of how the project would be graded at the same time as the assignment was given. In the remaining sections, the grading explanation was not given until just before groups were to give their presentations. Grading was described to the students to consist of three parts: One third of their grade would be based on instructor evaluation of their written presentation. One third of their grade would be based on project ratings from the members of other project groups. The final third would be based on both self-rating and other group members' ratings of each individual's level of effort toward completing the project.

All group oral presentations were done in the laboratory meetings of the class so that not all class members heard them all. The students in each section were asked to rank order the presentations in the section for the quality of the creative projects presented. That rank order was the dependent measure in the study (because the first author on this article was the course instructor, she was not blind to group condition and, therefore, her evaluation of the written presentations could not be used as the measure of group performance quality). In addition, the members of each project group completed written evaluation forms on which they rated the contribution of each member of the group to the project. They were asked to evaluate the extent to which each member "did their share of the work" using a 7-point Likert-type scale with anchors ranging from 1 (not at all) to 7 (very much so).

Operationalization of Hypothesis: Small Group Methods

Complete the following exercise in your group during the lab. You will present your answers in front of the class, and then have a discussion. Then, submit the form to your lab instructor.

Names of individuals in your group:

1. Original hypothesis:

2. If you were to use a small group research method for your study, how would you operationalize your hypothesis? Has this method ever been used to test hypotheses similar to yours? How? To what effect?

3. What are some possible benefits of using this method to test your hypothesis?

4. What are some possible limitations of using this method to test your hypothesis?

5. What ethical issues (if any) might you have if you used a small group research method to test your hypothesis? How might you overcome these issues? (*Hint: Have any other studies had to address these issues?*)

Draft of Introduction Section

For the next lab, you will need to submit a rough draft of your Introduction section. By now, you should have gathered a lot of literature for your Introduction, and have a clear set of hypotheses that you will be testing. You should just insert this text right into the outline that you already started.

Your Introduction must reference a minimum of five scientific papers, and should be at least three pages long (not including the references). For all of the citations you use in your paper, add them to the References section using APA formatting. Be sure to use APA format when citing them in the text of the paper as well.

Writing an Introduction

A good introduction can be difficult to write, because not only do you have to summarize and synthesize the existing research on your topic, but you also have to make a compelling case for carrying out your study. The introduction will also serve the purpose of presenting your primary hypotheses to the reader.

Below are some tips for writing a good introduction:

- Introduce the problem you intend to study in the first paragraph or two; be sure to highlight the importance of studying it.
- Summarize the relevant theories and studies that have influenced your approach to the problem. Only discuss past research that is directly relevant to the topic at hand.
  - Be sure to provide citations to specific research papers throughout the introduction.
- State your hypotheses. The hypotheses should be clear and appear reasonable, in light of the background literature you reviewed.
- Incorporate your study rationale that you wrote for lab #11

For additional information on writing an introduction, please consult the APA Publication Manual. You may also find the following website helpful:

http://owl.english.purdue.edu/owl/resource/670/04/

EVENT SAMPLING PROCEDURES

Lab #14

Purpose:

- Learn about event-sampling and other procedures to study daily experience.

Objectives:

- Review the following section entitled Event Sampling Procedures and discuss the rationale for utilizing this method in social psychological research.
- Learn about different types of research questions that can be answered with this procedure.
- Learn about types of experience (exemplary, ongoing, reconstructed) that can be sampled, and event types.
- Learn about how data are collected and recorded (interval-contingent, signal-contingent, and event-contingent).
- Learn about analysis issues with event-sampling.
- Read and discuss Method section excerpts using event-sampling methods from two published articles.
- Operationalize hypothesis using an event sampling methodology.

Homework:

- Submit another summary of an article for your Introduction.

Event Sampling Procedures

Event sampling (also known as experience sampling) is an approach to research that involves collecting data about participants' ongoing, daily experiences as they unfold in their natural environment. This is a radically different approach to research in the sense that the data are obtained entirely outside of an artificial laboratory setting. The study thus becomes a part of participants' everyday life for a set period of time. The end result is that researchers can obtain a much richer, more accurate, and (arguably) more realistic view of human behavior.

The exact implementation of event sampling varies widely from study to study. For instance, data may be captured regularly for a period of days or months, and participants may be submitting data only once per day or multiple times per day. In addition, the number and format of the questions may vary (i.e., fixed-choice vs. open-ended), and participants may be prompted to enter their responses in various ways (e.g., via an online survey accessed from a computer or via a smartphone application). Moreover, the study may be designed to capture participants' responses to relatively minor life events (e.g., everyday stressors), or they may be designed to reveal how participants respond to major life events (e.g., changes in marital or employment status). Regardless of how such studies are structured, they offer several unique advantages, including collection of data in a natural context,

fewer retrospective (i.e., memory) biases, and the ability to capture data that would be impossible to assess with other methodologies. In addition, such studies can serve multiple purposes, ranging from hypothesis testing, to establishing the prevalence of a given behavior, to simply discovering and describing what happens in "the real world."

It should be clear at this point that event sampling studies capture **ongoing experience**, with data collection focused on the reporting of thoughts, mood states, and behaviors as they happen from moment to moment. This is conceptually distinct from how most other social psychological research is carried out, given that most studies focus on either **exemplary experience** or **reconstructed experience**. Exemplary experience refers to data that are collected in some type of controlled environment (e.g., lab-based experiments), whereas reconstructed experience refers to data based upon participants' accounts of their own personal experiences. None of these approaches is necessarily better than the others. In fact, the reality is that they each reveal unique and valuable insights into our psychology and we are likely to obtain the best information about a given phenomenon to the extent that we utilize multiple methods of inquiry in a program of research.

Event sampling protocols generally take one of three forms (Wheeler & Reis, 1991): interval-contingent, signal-contingent, or event-contingent.

Interval-contingent protocols involve collecting data regularly at very specific time periods (e.g., every evening between 9:00 and 10:00 PM, or perhaps every 12 hours). At each time, participants may be asked to report on their current thoughts, feelings, and behaviors, or they may be asked to describe what changes have taken place since the last recording. **Signal-contingent protocols** involve prompting participants to input data any time a certain signal is communicated (e.g., a text message or computer alarm). Depending upon the specific study, the signals may occur at either fixed or random intervals. Random signals have the potential to yield more meaningful data than fixed signals because participants are unable to plan around them and intentionally alter their behavior. Finally, **event-contingent protocols** involve asking participants to report on specific events any time they happen. In order for this type of protocol to be successful, participants have to be perfectly clear on what the event is. In addition, the event cannot be something that happens so frequently that it becomes a pain to keep track of. As one example, consider a study by DePaulo, Kashy, Kirkendol, Wyer, and Epstein (1996) in which participants were asked to keep track of every lie they told over a one-week period. Participants were explicitly told that "a lie occurs any time you intentionally try to mislead someone. Both the intent to deceive and the actual deception must occur" (p. 981).

By defining "lie" in such specific terms, it helped to ensure more consistency in reporting both within and between participants.

Because the data provided by event sampling procedures are unique, we require unique analytic strategies in order to handle them. Perhaps the greatest complication with such datasets (aside from the large volume of data) is the fact that you cannot treat each time period, event, and signal as independent entities—rather, in studies of this nature, we have what is known as a nested data structure and our data points are non-independent. Analyzing nested data is complex and is well beyond the scope of what can be covered in this course. Thus, please keep in mind that conventional statistical procedures cannot necessarily be used to analyze data from all study designs.

References

DePaulo, B. M., Kashy, D. A., Kirkendol, S. E., Wyer, M. M., & Epstein, J. A. (1996). Lying in everyday life. *Journal of Personality and Social Psychology, 70,* 979. doi: 10.1037/0022-3514.70.5.979

Wheeler, L., & Reis, H. T. (1991). Self-recording of everyday life events: Origins, types, and uses. *Journal of Personality, 59,* 339-354. doi: 10.1111/j.1467-6494.1991.tb00252.x

The next pages are excerpts from two research articles using event-sampling research methods. You will read through these during class time and discuss.

The Value-Congruence Model of Memory for Emotional Experiences

An Explanation for Cultural Differences in Emotional Self-Reports

By Shigehiro Oishi, Ulrich Schimmack, Ed Diener, Chu Kim-Prieto, Christie Napa Scollon, and Dong-Won Choi

Study 3: Daily Event Sampling Study

O NE limitation of the scenario rating task used in Studies 1 and 2 is that emotional experiences assessed by this method were somewhat artificial because they were based on hypothetical situations. To address this limitation, in Study 3 we sampled the daily events that happened to participants in their lives and tested their memory for these real events. Participants recorded one positive and one negative event each day, as soon as the emotional episode ended, and rated how much they thought the event would make their parents happy and would lead to fulfillment of their parents' goals for them. We expected that the events that Asian Americans recalled later would be the events related to the fulfillment of their parents' goals for them, whereas the events that European Americans recalled would not be the events related to the fulfillment of their parents' goals for them. Furthermore, we examined whether the congruence effect between the cultural backgrounds and the type of events would be mediated by the individuals' value orientations, their independent and interdependent selves, and the importance of parental approval.

Method

Participants

Participants were 73 University of Illinois at Urbana-Champaign students who responded to the announcement of our study on campus. Of the original 73 participants, 29 self- identified European Americans (17 males, 12 females) and 26 self-identified Asian Americans (13 males, 13 females) completed the 3-week daily event study and recalled data at the end of the daily event study.

Procedure and Materials

Participants first completed a short survey that assessed their cultural backgrounds and value orientations. We measured value orientations, using the same scale used in Study 2 (i.e., rank order the 10 values, from 1 = *the least important* to 10 = *the most important*, as guiding principles of life) and the Self-Construal Scale (Singelis, 1994). The Self-Construal Scale consists of two 12-item subscales, the Independent Self (a = .72) and the Interdependent Self (a = .64), on which participants responded by using the 5-point scale (1 = *strongly disagree*, 5 = *strongly agree*). Finally,

Shigehiro Oishi, Ulrich Schimmack, Ed Diener, Chu Kim-Prieto, Christie Napa Scollon & Dong-Won Choi, "The Value-Congruence Model of Memory for Emotional Experiences: An Explanation for Cultural Differences in Emotional Self-Reports," *Journal of Personality and Social Psychology*, vol. 93, no. 5, pp. 901–902. Copyright © 2007 by American Psychological Association. Reprinted with permission.

participants rated the importance of each of the following domains on a 7-point scale (1 = *not at all important*; 7 = *extremely important*): happiness, life satisfaction, money, physical attractiveness, education, excitement, peace of mind, and parents' approval. The experimenter then explained to each participant how to use a personal digital assistant (PDA) to record each event and to complete a survey. Participants carried the PDA for 3 weeks and recorded one positive and one negative event each day, as soon as the event occurred. They briefly described what each event was and indicated the degree to which "this event will lead to fulfilling my parents' goals for me" and "this event will make my parents happy," on a 5-point scale (1 = *strongly disagree* to 5 = *strongly agree*). We took the average of responses to these two items to form the parental happiness score (a = .90). All the entries were time-stamped. Thus, we were able to verify that each event was indeed entered every day.

When participants completed the event sampling part of the study, they came back to the laboratory and performed a surprise recall test.

At this time, they were asked to recall as many of the events they recorded during the 3-week period as possible. Two independent judges who were blind to our hypotheses compared the list of recalled events with the events actually recorded. They were instructed to give a 0 for an event that was not recalled later, a 1 for an event that was recalled, and a .5 for an event that was recalled but for which the description was brief and was missing critical information (e.g., "I did poorly on my midterm exam" for the event originally described as "I did really bad on my chemistry midterm"). After achieving consensus on the first 20 events, two judges coded the rest of the 2,341 events independently. They reached a very high level of agreement (over 99%). Because the distribution of the recall score was highly skewed, we created a dichotomous score by classifying events with an average recall score of .75 or higher as 1 and classifying events with an average recall score of less than .75 as 0. In the following analyses involving the recall score, we used the Bernoulli model that has a binomial sampling model and a logit link in the model estimation.

When Accommodation Matters

Situational Dependency within Daily Interactions with Romantic Partners

By Nickola C. Overall and Chris G. Sibley

Method

Participants

PARTICIPANTS were 62 (46 females, 16 males) undergraduate psychology students studying at a New Zealand university who were involved in a romantic relationship and who reported regularly interacting with their romantic partner. Participants ranged from 17 to 37 years of age (M = 21.21, SD = 4.17) and received partial course credit for participation.

Procedure and Materials

Pre-diary questionnaire. Participants first completed 12 items from the Accommodation Scale developed by Rusbult et al. (1991). Three items assessed the tendency to react to dependency-related situations (e.g., negative partner behavior) with exit-based responses, for example "When my partner is rude and inconsiderate with me, I think about ending our relationship" (M = 3.05, SD = 1.59, a = .93). Three items assessed the tendency to use voice-based responses when faced with dependency dilemmas, for example "When my partner yells at me or speaks in a raised voice, I calmly discuss things with my partner" (M =6.26, SD = 1.43, a = .81). Three items assessed the tendency to respond with

loyalty, for example "When my partner is angry with me and ignores me for awhile, I give my partner the benefit of the doubt and forget about it" (M =4.26, SD =1.54, a = .73), and three items assessed the tendency to respond with neglect, for example "When my partner yells at me or speaks in a raised voice, I ignore the whole thing and try to spend less time with my partner" (M = 3.89, SD = 1.26, a = .67). Items were rated on a scale ranging from 1 (never do this) through a midpoint of 4 (sometimes do this) to 9 (constantly do this). In line with prior research (e.g., Rusbult et al., 1991; Rusbult, Bissonnette, et al., 1998; Wieselquist et al., 1999), we constructed an overall measure of the tendency to accommodate by reverse scoring self-protective destructive items (i.e., exit and neglect) and then averaging scores across the four types of responses. In general, participants reported moderate levels of general accommodation behavior (M = 5.90, SD = .87).

Relationship satisfaction was assessed using 4 items from the scale developed by Rusbult, Martz, and Agnew (1998), for example, "All things considered, I feel satisfied with our relationship," and "Our relationship is close to ideal" (1 = strongly disagree, 9 = strongly agree). On average, participants reported reasonably high levels of relationship satisfaction (M = 7.75, SD = .97, a = .80).

Social interaction diary. Participants completed a variant of Wheeler and Nezlek's

(1977) social interaction diary for the next 14 consecutive days. Participants were asked to record a diary entry for every instance in which they interacted with another person or persons for 10 min or longer. A detailed tutorial outlined instructions for completing the diary accurately. The importance of updating the diary as often as possible in order to improve the accuracy of ratings was stressed, and participants were asked to complete the diary a minimum of two or three times a day. Participants were also contacted after the first week in order to assess their performance and answer any additional queries.

Each social interaction diary record contained the standard descriptive measures outlined by Wheeler and Nezlek (1977, e.g., date, time, number and gender of interactants, etc.). Participants indicated their relationship to each interactant (e.g., romantic partner, family member, friend, acquaintance, colleague, et al.). If the interaction involved two or more people, then participants listed these people in order according to the amount of time and attention they gave to each person during the interaction. The social interactions in which a romantic partner was listed as the primary interactant formed the data set analyzed here.

Participants then rated the extent to which they felt accepted and valued during the interaction (1 = not at all accepted/valued, 7 = totally accepted/valued) and the degree to which they experienced intimacy within the interaction (1 = not at all intimate, 7 = very intimate). Ratings of these two items were combined to form an aggregate measure of perceived value and intimacy.[1]

Participants also rated their level of influence and control within the interaction (1 = no influence/control, 7 = total influence/control). As outlined in the introduction, this is a good index of felt dependency because the extent to which individuals are dependent within interactions with their romantic partners will be at its peak when individuals can not exert influence or control.

Operationalization of Hypothesis: Event Sampling Methods

Complete the following exercise with your group during the lab. You will present your answers in front of the class, and then have a discussion. Then, submit the form to your lab instructor.

Names of individuals in your group:

1. Original hypothesis:

2. If you were to use an event sampling method for your study, how would you operationalize your hypothesis? Has this method ever been used to test hypotheses similar to yours? How? To what effect?

3. What are some possible benefits of using this method to test your hypothesis?

4. What are some possible limitations of using this method to test your hypothesis?

5. What ethical issues (if any) might you have if you used an event sampling research method to test your hypothesis? How might you overcome these issues? (*Hint: Have any other studies had to address these issues?*)

Homework Assignment: Summary of Additional Article for the Introduction

B Y now, you have read a lot of background material for your study, and have submitted an initial draft of your Introduction. As you write and revise your paper, you will need to conduct additional literature reviews using PsycINFO, in order to provide more background support and/ or build on your rationale for your study. For this assignment, you will conduct another literature search on your research topic to bolster your paper.

1. Generate a number of search terms that you will use for your literature search. These can be key words from your primary article, the author's name, a research topic or method contained within the article, etc.
2. Go on to the PsycINFO search engine through the library website, and use your search terms to generate a list of articles, chapters, etc.
3. Read through titles and abstracts that look most interesting to you. Select one new article. For this assignment, this could be a research article, a literature review, or a theoretical paper. Be sure that your new article is different from your re-search team members' articles. *If there are any duplicates, you will not receive credit for your summary.*
4. Get the article from the library and read it.
5. Next, you will prepare a summary of the article that you will turn in to your instructor and lab

group members. Your summary should be in the following format:

I. Background of the study:
  Give a reference citation (be sure to use APA format *exactly*).
  Goal/purpose of the paper.
II. Method or overview of the theory:
  Research article
    Participants/materials/measures used.
    Procedure.
    Results.
  Theory/review
    Key constructs of topic identified.
    Specific postulates of the theory or work outlined.
III. Study Relevance:
  State how this study is important, and relevant/related to your research topic.

Your summary should be at least one page long, double spaced, using 12-point font. Print a copy for each member of your research team (including yourself), and one for your instructor to bring to the next lab.

QUALITATIVE PROCEDURES

Lab #15

Purpose:

- Learn about content and narrative procedures in social psychology.

Objectives:

- Review the following section entitled Qualitative Methods and discuss the rationale for utilizing these procedures in social psychological research.
- Learn about different types of research questions that can be answered with these procedures.
- Learn the steps involved in content research and how to code data.
- Learn how to approach narrative analyses.
- Read and discuss Method section excerpts using event-sampling methods from two published articles.
- Complete in-class qualitative analysis activity.
- Operationalize hypothesis using content analysis.
- Select operationalization for your study.

Homework:

- Submit rationale for the operationalization to be used in your study.
- Submit revision of Introduction section and draft of Methods section.
- Study for quiz labs #13–15.

Qualitative Methods

THE research methods covered so far in this book have primarily focused on empirical methods that provide data in numerical form. For example, in survey research, you might request attitude ratings toward a particular group using a scale ranging from 1-5. Alternatively, in psychophysiological research, you might measure heart rate during exposure to various stimuli. In comparison, qualitative methods involve collecting and analyzing non-numeric data.

What does non-numeric data look like? Such data can take many forms, from audio transcripts of interviews, to focus group discussions, to written responses to open ended survey questions (e.g., *"Describe what you do in a typical day"*), to newspaper headlines over several months of years, to diaries or books written centuries ago. There are many ways one can gather qualitative data.

One criticism that has been raised about qualitative research is that the sampling of data is **purposive** instead of random, the latter of which is considered the "ideal" for quantitative research. Purposive sampling means that the participants or sources are selected because they are believed to provide the most useful data. In other words, you would select people to interview who have had a certain experience, and then try and get as much variability within that sample as possible. For example, imagine that you wanted to interview people about their attitudes toward a new highway

that is going to be built in their community. You would purposefully select people that would be directly impacted by this new construction, and you would find a diverse array of people who may be differentially affected, such as business owners, police, home owners, and so forth. Sample sizes are generally small in qualitative studies because there is often a wealth of complex data generated by each source. Having too many data points is therefore next to impossible to analyze. The goal with such data is to reach what is called **saturation**, which is the point at which you start hearing the same themes being discussed repeatedly by participants, and no new information comes out.

There are a number of reasons researchers might use qualitative methods to answer their research questions. For one thing, this approach allows for much greater diversity of responses from participants. For example, if you were collecting numeric data, you might simply ask participants in a survey to rate how intimate they feel with their romantic partner (e.g., 1 = *not intimate at all* to *7 = very intimate*). In contrast, if you were collecting non-numeric data, you could ask people to describe what intimacy in their relationship looks or feels like in their own words. In the latter case, the researcher can assess how the participant subjectively defines what intimacy means, and gauge intimacy based upon how the relationship is described. The simple survey question is nice in that it provides data along a continuum, but you would not really have a sense of what intimacy might mean for each individual person in that scenario. Therefore, qualitative data can potentially provide richer data than quantitative data.

Qualitative data are also useful when you are investigating a new research question or conducting research with a new population, such as psychologists who work in cross-cultural contexts. Rather than asking *how many* and *how much* questions, qualitative researchers ask questions such as *what*, *how*, and *why*. Asking people what their experiences and perspectives are related to a particular problem can bring to light issues and ideas that the researcher would not have thought of on their own. Science cannot be entirely objective because researchers generate research questions based on their own perspectives, cultural backgrounds, and values. Therefore, conducting qualitative research can provide a way for other populations to give voice to their issues and concerns. In other words, rather than have a researcher assume that they know what the important factors are, the sample will reveal them on their own. This bottom-up approach can therefore generate novel research ideas, and inform the researcher about the generalizability of theoretical concepts to other populations. As one example, we (Harman and Lehmiller) recently conducted a large scale survey of polyamorous individuals (individuals who have open, consensual loving relationships with more than one person). We asked participants to describe, in their own words, what *commitment* means to them. We did this instead of asking them how committed they are using a standard definition of "commitment," which typically includes an element of exclusivity. We thought that nonmonogamous persons might have a rather different take on this concept. Indeed, we found that in this population, commitment meant many different things (e.g., loyalty), but exclusivity was rarely one of them.

One drawback of conducting qualitative analyses is that it can be expensive and very time consuming. Imagine that you interview 20 people for 60 minutes each. You would have to record the interview, transcribe it, and then conduct a thorough coding of the data. This can take a considerable amount of time, and requires extensive training of all coders (one coder is generally not sufficient to ensure reliability of interpretation). Alternatively, imagine that you wanted to conduct an archival analysis of TV news broadcasts related to the terrorist attacks of 9/11 in the United States. You would need to identify which news sources you would pull from (i.e., your population), describe how you would randomly sample from the population to make for manageable coding, create a coding scheme that would address your research question, and then code and interpret the results. Thus, while some individuals think that qualitative analyses are "easy" compared to the analysis of quantitative data, this is a major misconception.

Analyzing qualitative data is complicated, and the many techniques that are available are well beyond the scope of this introductory manual to cover. Most strategies involve reading through or listening to the data and getting a feel for the general themes that emerge. Then, more careful coding is conducted using categorical schemes developed by the researcher. You may code for the mention of certain words, for common statements or issues raised by particular informants, and so on. What is coded is specifically related to the research question. As with behavioral observation, you ideally should have more than one coder so that the coders can compare their results and look for discrepancies. There are also some software programs that are useful for the analysis of qualitative data (e.g., iAtlas), in which you simply input different themes or words, and the software searches in your text file for any time the search terms are mentioned. After themes and other important characteristics are identified, researchers must then interpret the data in relation to their initial research question.

The next pages are excerpts from two research articles using content analysis research methods. You will read through these during class time and discuss.

Dimensions of Majority and Minority Groups

By Viviane Seyranian, Hazel Atuel, and William D. Crano

Method

Participants

SEVENTY-SEVEN participants were recruited from classes at a junior college and a university in Southern California. Approximately 60% of the sample was female. Participants' ages ranged from 18–47 years (M = 26, SD = 7.5). Participants' ethnicity was comparable to California's ethnic distribution, as reported by the United States Census Bureau (2000). European-Americans comprised 40% of the sample, followed by Hispanics/Latinos (29%), Asians/Pacific Islanders (15%), African-Americans (9%), and other ethnicities (7%). Most participants rated themselves as middle class (73%) or working class/poor (24%), with only a few in the upper class (3%).

Materials

All participants completed a survey that asked for descriptors of majority and minority groups, along with standard demographic information about the participants themselves. The descriptors of majority and minority groups were contained in two separate sections of the survey. Each section contained 10 fill-in-the-blank sentence stems. One section was devoted to describing the minority (10 stems), the other section to describing the majority (10 stems). The order of majority and minority descriptors was counterbalanced across participants.[1]

Majority and minority descriptors. To measure their perceptions of majority and minority groups, participants completed sentence stems that read: "A majority (or minority) is ____ because ____ which is a positive/negative thing." The instructions for completing the majority (or minority section) were as follows:

This section asks you to fill-in-the-blanks about your views concerning majority (or minority) groups. There are 10 such sentences in this section. Please complete as many as you possibly can. For each one, in the first blank, please write down a word that describes a minority (or majority) group. In the second blank, provide a brief description of why the word appropriately characterizes a minority (or majority) group. Finally, circle a positive or negative value attached to the description. Remember, there is no right or wrong answer.

Because the current study sought to explore group definitions, only the first part of the descriptor ("A majority is ____") was coded and analyzed. The second part ("because ____") provided a coding context that helped to clarify the meaning of the first part (see Crano & Brewer, 2002) when participants' answers were ambiguous or not easily coded (e.g., "A minority is *an exploited group* because *they are singled out for unequal treatment.*").

Approximately 87% of participants completed 5 or fewer descriptors for the majority (M = 3.31) and 75% completed the same for the minority (M = 4.29). In fact, only one participant was able to provide 10 majority descriptors and only three provided 10 minority descriptors. Clearly, future research employing this measure may not need to include as many sentence stems.

Valence. The third part (circling "which is a negative/positive thing") of the sentence stem measured the *valence* of majority and minority descriptors. Valence was calculated by summing the positive and negative values assigned to relevant descriptors. Composite valence scores could range from -10 (10 negative descriptors) to +10. Each participant produced two valence scores, one for majorities and another for minorities.

Salience. Tajfel and Wilkes (1963) suggested that an attribute is salient to the extent that it is frequent (used often) and prioritized (the first of a series). The salience of majority and minority descriptors was operationalized by considering the first descriptors that participants listed for each type of group.

Fluency and flexibility. *Fluency* refers to the number of ideas a person generates. It was operationalized by summing the total number of descriptors each participant produced for majority and for minority groups. Every participant thus had two fluency scores, each ranging from 0 (low fluency) to 10 (high fluency). *Flexibility* refers to the total number of unique ideas someone generates. It was oper- ationalized by summing the total number of unique dimensions used to describe majority and minority groups. A participant who

listed five descriptors for majority groups, three of which were coded as power, one as number, and one as dispositions, would thus receive a score of 3 for majority group flexibility (1 for each of 3 group dimensions). Flexibility scores could range from 0 (inflexible) to 9 (high flexibility) for each type of group.

Demographic variables. The final measures involved participants' age, sex, ethnicity, socio-economic status, and religious affiliation.

Procedure

Data collection. Students were recruited from various university and college classes. At the end of each class session, the instructor introduced one of the authors and left the classroom. The investigator gave students the cover story that they were to complete a survey on their personal beliefs related to certain groups. Students were informed that their participation in the study was voluntary and that they were free to leave if they chose not to participate. Only one student (out of 78) opted not to participate in the study. Students who chose to participate were given the option to take part in a lottery to receive a US$25 gift certificate (three gift certificates were allotted for each class). Next, participants were asked if they had any questions about the study. The only question raised in all of the classes concerned the length of the survey, which the investigator estimated would take approximately 15–25 minutes. Students were told, however, that they could take as much time as they needed.

After any student questions were answered, participants were given the survey and those who wished to participate in the lottery were assigned lottery numbers. The investigator stayed in the back of the classroom while participants completed their surveys (working on their own). When they were done, usually after 15 to 30 minutes, participants turned in their questionnaires and returned to their seats. Prior to dismissal, participants were fully debriefed about the nature of the study and told that the survey was designed to assess definitions of majority and minority groups. No participant was able to identify any of our research questions. Subsequently, gift certificates were raffled and presented to the winning students. All students then were dismissed.

Coding procedure. Prior to examining and coding the descriptors, we established a provisional coding list of possible group dimensions (Miles & Huberman, 1994) based on prior literature. The provisional list included five dimensions: number, power, opinions, distinctiveness, and ingroup-outgroup status. After an initial review of participants' responses, the provisional list was revised. Six more dimensions were added (social categories, group context, target treatment, source treatment, dispositions, and other), and two of the initial dimensions were dropped (opinions, ingroup-outgroup status). Using the final coding scheme, which included nine group dimensions, one of the authors coded all of the data. A naive independent assistant also coded all of the descriptors. There was substantial intercoder agreement (Cohen's kappa = .88 for majority and .87 for minority descriptors). The first coder's scores were used in all of the analyses.

The Motivational Basis of Concessions and Compromise

Archival and Laboratory Studies

By Carrie A. Langner and David G. Winter

Study 1: Developing and Validating a Coding System for Concessions

WHAT is a concession, and how can it be measured in both archival and laboratory research? On the one hand, the diplomatic history literature contains many examples but few precise operational definitions or procedures for quantification. On the other hand, laboratory researchers often measure concessions by seemingly superficial variables such as the giving or exchanging of small sums of money or "points." Although these measures are precise, they do not necessarily have anything to do with concessions in the real world of international relations (or, for that matter, even significant interpersonal relationships). For the present research, therefore, we decided to construct a new measure of concession making that could be used in both archival and laboratory studies.

Measuring Concessions: A Grounded Theory Approach

On the basis of a review of the political and psychological literature (e.g., Etzioni, 1967; Kriesberg & Thorson, 1991, pp. 264–265), as well as intensive comparison of diplomatic documents from a crisis that escalated to war and a similar crisis that was peacefully resolved,

Langner (1997) first developed a system for coding concessions on the basis of verbal content. The two crises were the outbreak of war between the United States and Mexico and the peaceful settlement of the U.S. dispute with Great Britain about the Oregon boundary. Both were related to the American sense of Manifest Destiny and territorial expansion to the Pacific Coast, both were handled by the administration of President James K. Polk, and both occurred during 1845 and the first half of 1846 (see Winter, 1997).

The concessions scoring system is organized in terms of four positive categories and four parallel negative categories. The positive categories all involve proposing or accepting concessions in a dispute:

1. Proposals for procedural arrangements that will facilitate negotiation and peaceful resolution of a crisis;
2. Suggestions or offers of mediation by some third party (cf. Rubin, 1981);
3. Taking, or offering to take, some specific act of de-escalation (can be subdivided into unilateral and reciprocal de-escalation acts); and
4. Accepting a concession (Categories 1–3 above) made by the other side.

The negative categories are parallel to the positive ones, but involve rejecting concessions or escalating conflict:

1. Declining or rejecting a procedural proposal made by the other side;
2. Refusing a suggestion or offer of mediation;
3. Taking, or threatening to take, some specific act of escalation (can be subdivided into unilateral and reciprocal escalation); and
4. Rejecting a proposed concession (positive Category 3 above) made by the other side.

Further definitions and examples of these categories are given in Table 2. In applying the system, the sentence is the unit of scoring. The eight categories are logically independent of each other, which means that, in principle, each sentence could be scored for the presence of any category or categories.

Cross-Validating the Concessions Measure in Archival Documents from Four Crises

The first study was designed for two purposes: (a) to establish the real-world validity of the concessions scoring system and (b) to explore the relationships between affiliation and power-motive imagery and concessions. To cross-validate the scoring system, diplomatic documents and other written government-to-government communications from two additional pairs of crises were mixed together and blindly scored for concessions and motive imagery. Each pair consisted of a peacefully resolved crisis and a similar crisis (involving approximately the same countries, during the same historical era) that escalated to armed conflict. This method has been characterized by George (1979) as structured focused comparison (or disciplined configurative), which is a type of historically grounded theory development: Comparable individual cases, with different outcomes, are described, analyzed, and explained in terms of theoretically relevant general variables.

The first matched pair consisted of the 1938 crisis over German demands to annex parts of Czechoslovakia, which was peacefully resolved at the Munich series of conferences among Germany, Great Britain, France, and Italy that averted (perhaps unwisely, and in any case only for a few months) war. It was paired with the 1939 crisis over German demands to annex Danzig and modify the German-Polish boundary. That crisis ended on September 1, 1939, with the outbreak of World War II, as Germany invaded Poland. Both of these crises arose from German expansion and involved Great Britain and Germany as major antagonists. The other matched pair consisted of two crises over Cuba that involved the United States and the former Soviet Union: the disastrous 1961 Bay of Pigs invasion of Cuba by Cuban exiles, who were in fact organized, financed, and directed by the United States (Fursenko & Naftali, 1997), and the October 1962 Cuban Missile Crisis, in which the United States and Soviet Union narrowly averted nuclear war. Although the Bay of Pigs lasted for only a few days, it was clearly a war, complete with bombing, aerial combat, and intense ground fighting between the Cuban army and the American-trained and American-supplied invaders.

The first hypothesis of the archival study is that the documents from the two peacefully resolved crises will score higher in total and positive concessions and lower in negative concessions than documents from the two war crises. The second hypothesis is that across all documents, the number of positive concessions will be positively correlated with affiliation motivation and negatively correlated with power motivation and that for negative concessions, these correlations will be reversed.

Method

Selection of Documents

The first step we took was to establish precise beginning and ending dates. On the basis of the discussion in Watt (1989), the Munich crisis was considered to have begun on May 22, 1938, and ended on September 29, 1938, whereas the Poland crisis began on March 31, 1939 and ended on September 3, 1939. Dates for the Bay of Pigs (April 6–22, 1961) and Cuban Missile Crisis (October 22–28, 1962) were based on the dates of the first and last documents available for scoring.

For each crisis, all documents representing official government public statements or government-to-government communications were drawn from the collection of documents assembled by Winter (1997) from published archival sources (see Appendix A for a list of all documents). This yielded 32 written government-to-government communications for the Munich crisis and 16 for Poland (taken from U.S. Department of State, 1949, and Woodward & Butler, 1949–1954). For the two U.S.–Soviet crises involving Cuba, the written government-to-government communications (from U.S. Department of State, 1973) were supplemented by two public statements by President John F. Kennedy (one speech and one press conference transcript) and three official Soviet public statements, for a total of seven Bay of Pigs documents and 12 Cuban Missile Crisis documents. Within each of the paired crises, the documents used were comparable: verbatim government-to-government communications for Munich and Poland and government-to-government communications plus public statements for the Bay of Pigs and Cuban Missile Crisis.

To the extent that we were able to match both the nature of the crises and the type of documents scored within each pair, within-pair differences can be attributed (whether as cause or effect) to the different outcomes—peace or war—of the two crises.

Scoring of Documents

Documents from all four crises were mixed together in random order and scored for concessions by two scorers who had been trained by Carrie Langner. To avoid bias, scoring of concessions was done by two scorers who were unaware of the purpose and hypotheses of the research and who had little knowledge of the four specific crises. The scorers were trained in the use of the scoring system by Langner.

On a portion of these documentary materials that had also been scored by Langner, these two scorers attained category agreement figures (see Smith, 1992, p. 529) with Langner of .75 and .63. Both scorers scored all documents, resolving all disagreements after discussion. Because the documents varied in length, the raw concessions scores for each document were divided by the number of words and multiplied by 1,000 to give a figure of concessions per 1,000 words. Finally, subtracting negative concessions from positive concessions scores gave a net concessions score.

These documents had previously been scored for affiliation and power-motive imagery according to the integrated running-text scoring system (Winter, 1991) as a part of Winter's (1997) study, by a trained scorer who was blind to the hypotheses and the historical details of the crises and who had previously demonstrated high reliability (category agreement > .85) on materials precoded by expert scorers. Scores for each motive were also expressed in terms of images per 1,000 words. To avoid the theoretical issue of whether impersonal documents or their collective authors can have motives or motivation (as individual persons do; see Winter, 1993), as well as the conceptual status of the motive imagery measures, we used the theoretically more neutral term motive imagery to refer to these scores.

In-Class Qualitative Analysis

For this exercise, you are to meet with your research group. You will analyze a five-minute video clip for evidence of violence. First, you are to define what the terms "mildly violent" and "severely violent" acts mean. Then, you are to independently code the video clip. Last, you are to reconvene with your group and compare your responses.

Definitions:

Mildly Violent Acts:
screaming

Severely Violent Acts:
anything physical

Characters	Mildly Violent Acts	Severely Violent Acts
Michelle	ⅢⅡ ⅢⅡ Ⅲ	ⅢⅡ

Total Mild Acts____13____
Total Severe Acts____7____
Total Acts____20____

Operationalization of Hypothesis: Content Analysis Method

COMPLETE the following exercise in your group during the lab. You will present your answers in front of the class, and then have a discussion. Then, submit the form to your lab instructor.

Names of individuals in your group:

1. Original hypothesis:

When an individual is exposed to a stressful scenario of job loss during COVID-19, individuals are more likely to utilize problem focused coping

2. If you were to use a content analysis method for your study, how would you operationalize your hypothesis? Has this method ever been used to test hypotheses similar to yours? How? To what effect?

If we were to use a content analysis for our study we would operationalize our hypothesis by looking at two groups where one is economically effected by the pandemic and those who were not. I would have both groups keep a diary to track their emotions and explain how they coped. A study like this has not been conducted yet.

3. What are some possible benefits of using this method to test your hypothesis?

A benefit of this style is that participants can use their own words so therefore are not subject to a scale. This type of study, being completely subjective makes the diversity of responses greater. From the diversity of the response can also lead to new research questions. We can also utilize this cross culturally to see how other adults from different countries deal with job loss during covid-19.

4. What are some possible limitations of using this method to test your hypothesis?

A possible limiting of using this method is how complex the data may turn out to be. A diary is robust information and is a lot to read and difficult to operationally define. Following a diary is also very time consuming and hiring multiple coders for interrater reliability can be expensive

5. What ethical issues (if any) might you have if you used a content analysis method to test your hypothesis? How might you overcome these issues? (*Hint: Have any other studies had to address these issues?*)

The only ethical issue we might have if we used content analysis is the idea of intruding on people's personal lives. Individuals may not want researchers to read a diary about their emotions on losing their job. A way we could overcome this is telling them it is purely for research and the betterment of society and that they will remain confidential and will just be identified as an identification number

Rationale for Method Selected for the Study

Your lab group should complete the following form, and turn it in to your lab instructor by the next lab meeting. Write your responses below.

1. Which method have you decided to use for your study?

2. Why did you select this method instead of the other methods (be specific)? In other words, why have you decided on this method rather than the other methods that you considered?

3. How do you plan on addressing the limitations of this method you chose in your study? (Please reference #5 of the operationalization worksheets for this method.)

Revision to Introduction and Draft of Method Section

For your next lab, you must also submit a revision to your Introduction section, based on the feedback you received. You should also include the last draft with this current one, so that your instructor can be sure that you made the suggested changes. Be certain to also add information from the last article that you summarized!

In addition, you will submit a draft of your Method section.

Writing a Method Section

The Method section is perhaps the most straightforward section of the paper to write, because APA style dictates that it should be broken up into several specific subheadings. None of the other major sections in an APA-style paper are as rigidly structured.

A Method section is usually divided into the following parts:

- *Participants.* This section describes who is going to participate in your study, and addresses demographic features of the sample (e.g., participants' age, race, gender).
- *Research Design.* This section is typically only included if you are conducting an experiment. You would describe the independent and dependent variables here. For a correlational study, you could omit this subsection entirely.

- *Measures/Materials.* This section describes all of the tests and measures you plan to include in your research. You should describe each measure separately, cite the original source, and provide sample items.
- *Procedure.* This section describes the data collection procedure(s) in detail. At a minimum, you will address how participants will be recruited; informed consent procedures; what participants will be asked to do during the study; and debriefing procedures. Based on your description, another researcher should be able to replicate your study exactly—without needing to contact you for information on what you did.

One general point to keep in mind is that this section will be written in the future tense for your initial draft(s), because you have yet to collect your data (e.g., "Participants will be 50 college student participants, with approximately equal numbers of men and women."). However, for your final paper, you will change this and all other sections to the past tense, given that the study will be completed at this time (e.g., "Participants were 50 college student participants made up of 26 women and 24 men.").

For additional information on writing and formatting a Method section, please consult the APA Publication Manual. You may also find the following website helpful:

- http://owl.english.purdue.edu/owl/resource/670/04/

INSTITUTIONAL REVIEW BOARDS

Lab #16

Purpose:

- Learn about Institutional Review Boards (IRBs) at universities, and how to obtain IRB approval for research.

Objectives:

- Take quiz on labs #13–15.
- Review the following section entitled Institutional Review Boards. Discuss why we have IRBs, the review process, and what documentation is usually needed for IRB approval.

Homework:

- Complete measurement worksheet.
- Complete online ethics training. This training will take a while to complete, but is necessary for all researchers to conduct their studies. If you have already completed this training within the last three years, you can just provide the certificate as proof to your instructor. Once you create a profile, you can log in at a later point and finish when you have time. Print up the certificate at the end of the training and bring it to the next lab session, where we will discuss the IRB process. The website for the training is https://www.citiprogram.org/Default.asp?
- Be sure to take the Social Sciences Ethics training, and register as a student or research assistant.

Institutional Review Boards

Why We Have Them and How They Work

THERE are many historical examples of social psychological research studies that were unethical either by design, execution, or analysis (e.g., Milgram's classic experiments on obedience to authority). Obviously, social psychology as a discipline was not the only culprit here; researchers in many other fields were also guilty (e.g., medicine). However, due to growing concerns about how research participants were being treated in studies, federal laws were eventually passed in order to protect their rights.

Implementation of these laws was ultimately delegated to what are termed Institutional Review Boards or IRBs (also called ethical review boards, independent ethics committees, etc., depending on the type of institution). These review boards are charged with approving and monitoring research projects involving human subjects. IRBs function under a group process, whereby either the entire board or a few members will review all proposals and related materials (e.g., informed consent documents, surveys) developed by researchers to determine whether human rights and welfare are being protected.

Who can be a member of an IRB? Federal regulations require that IRBs be a diverse group of at least five individuals with varying levels of expertise and cultural backgrounds (e.g., race, gender, age). At least one member must have some scientific expertise in an area related to the proposal, and at least one member must have expertise in a non-scientific area. Sometimes

IRBs will hire consultants to ensure that they have people who can review proposals objectively from their perspective. For example, if you were to conduct research with prisoners, you should have an IRB member who has worked with a prisoner or ex-offender population. The board members should be able to evaluate the scientific merit of research proposals, the sensitivity of the study to the community in which the work is being conducted, whether the study complies with federal laws and regulations, as well as standards of practice.

There are several types of reviews that an IRB can conduct to evaluate research. **Full review** is conducted when the research may pose a significant risk to participants (e.g., deception is used) or when research is conducted with vulnerable populations (e.g., prisoners, minors, pregnant women). **Expedited review** is reserved for proposals that pose minimal ethical risks to participants. For example, let us say that you wanted to conduct a survey of consumer preferences for Coke vs. Pepsi without collecting any identifying information from participants. People participate in surveys of this nature all of the time via online "quick polls" and marketing calls, so there is nothing unusual or especially risky about your procedure. The minimal risk associated with such a study would mean that it would not need to receive full IRB review by all board members. Expedited reviews can also happen when a researcher just wants to make a minor change to an existing protocol, and this change does not alter risk for participants. Finally, **exempt review** is reserved for studies that pose almost no risk to participants and are part of what would happen naturally in a particular setting. For example, you might request exempt review for a study of archival data from deceased participants that have no identifying information attached to the records. Alternatively, you might be able to request exempt review if you were simply going to observe people's natural behavior in a shopping mall.

What do IRBs look for when they evaluate proposals? First, they want to ensure that you have minimized all possible risks to participants. To accomplish this, you need a solid understanding of research methods and you must carefully think through all aspects of the study; for example, online surveys may sound simple and harmless, but there are ethical issues associated with their use (e.g., will you be collecting IP addresses from participants' computers, which could be personally identifying?). IRBs also look to see whether the potential benefits of the research outweigh the potential risks. To that end, you must do a very good job of communicating the practical and theoretical importance of conducting your study. If the benefits are great, this can justify some of the risk that participants may be exposed to. IRBs also look to ensure that the selection of participants is equitable. We cannot just decide to exclude certain classes of people (e.g., minors) without a scientifically-based or justifiable reason.

IRBs also want to make sure that informed consent will be collected from participants appropriately. Researchers must be able to make the case to the IRB that the population they are studying has the capacity to make an informed decision. If participants are minors or have mental disabilities, then their ability to make an informed choice is limited and extra precautions must be taken (e.g., you may need to obtain written consent from the participants' legal guardians). In contrast, when a study poses minimal risk, the IRB may not require you to collect signed consent forms and instead

allow you to present a cover letter explaining the nature of the study. In addition to proper consent procedures, IRBs look to ensure that the data collected will be kept safe and protected, so that the confidentiality of participants is protected.

After approval from the IRB, researchers are responsible for monitoring their study for deviations from the approved protocol and documenting cases where participants were harmed or complaints were received. All incidents must be reported to the IRB, along with a description of how the issues were remedied (e.g., change in protocol, a cancellation of the study). At a minimum, researchers are required to provide yearly reports to the IRB, as well as a notice when the study is completed.

What happens when people violate federal law and run studies without IRB approval, or conduct the study differently than was approved? Professional journals and other dissemination outlets often will not publish the data, all data collected may be confiscated, the researcher may need to contact all participants and offer an opportunity to correct any negative outcomes, the researcher may be censured (e.g., banned from conducting research for a period of time), and sometime the institution itself may lose its ability to conduct and oversee any research at all for a period of time. As you can see, violations are a serious issue.

Although each educational institution may have its own policies, most research conducted for classroom experience (e.g., as part of a lab experience like this one) does not require formal IRB approval, but does require very close instructor supervision. Regardless of whether you are required to get IRB approval or not, it is important to get experience thinking through the kinds of ethical issues that IRBs require to get a thorough understanding of the research process. That is why we devote a considerable amount of time in this book to thinking through these issues and practice writing a proposal for "IRB approval," whether that approval is from your instructor, a mock IRB, or a real one.

Measurement Worksheet

Now that you have decided how to operationalize your hypothesis, your next step is to decide how it will be measured, and what instruments you will use. To complete this worksheet, work with your teammates to answer the following questions thoroughly. You may want to reference your lecture notes from lab #7. They will help you when we start writing IRB protocols in the next lab. You may need multiple pages to answer these questions, depending on the number of constructs, variables, and instruments you decide to use!

1. What is your hypothesis?

2. What are the constructs that you are interested in?

3. What are the variables?

4. How can you measure the variables?

5. What instruments will you use to measure your variables (provide references for them)?

Lab #17

Purpose:

- Learn about how to draft consent forms, cover sheets, debriefing materials, and IRB materials for the study.

Objectives:

- Work on IRB forms for mock IRB approval in class. Review the following sections and sample forms to learn more about the materials you will need to create.

Homework:

- None!

IRB Materials

For the next phase of your research project, you and your teammates must develop your materials for IRB review. You will have to first turn in your **IRB protocol** (this form and the instructions are included on the following pages) and **a cover letter, debriefing, and recruitment materials** (see models that follow). Believe it or not, by doing this exercise, you will be writing the basis of your final research paper, as well as fine-tuning the procedures of your study.

After you create your IRB materials with your group, your instructor will provide you with his or her own feedback and/or request feedback from other faculty members in the department. This mock IRB will make comments on your proposals, and require additional changes before you are approved to run your experiment. When you submit this material, you must also include the **measures and recruitment statement** that you will be using in your experiment. **Make sure that the answers you give to the questions on the IRB form match the content of your cover letter, debriefing form, surveys, etc**. Also, if you plan on recruiting from a classroom, be specific about which ones, and **provide evidence that you have obtained instructor approval**.

NOTE: Many students use the words "random" or "randomly" inappropriately in their proposals. For example, many students indicate that they plan to "Randomly interview students in front of ____." This is not a random sample, it is a convenience sample. Recall that random selection means that every person in the target population has an equal chance of being approached or selected to participate in your study. Some students also inappropriately use the word in examples such as this: "Random questions will be asked of participants, such as age and gender." These are not random questions at all. In other words, avoid using the word "random" unless you mean that people or items have an equal chance of being selected or assigned to a group.

Recruiting Materials. If you are advertising your study to a class, around campus, or online, you need to submit a recruitment statement with your materials. This statement should contain a shortened version of the cover letter's material. Tell the people who you are; what the project is for; why they are being recruited; and what would be required of them. It is more or less an "invitation" to participate. Typically, it is only a few sentences long.

Debriefing Materials. This should contain the content of what your debriefing contains. Some of you will conduct a verbal debriefing, some a written one. The IRB needs to see what will be covered. The debriefing should thank the participant for her or his help, and then more thoroughly explain the study, and your hypotheses. Tell them what you expect to find, and why the study is important. Ask whether they have any questions, and thank them again. It should also refer participants to the Principal Investigator (PI; whose information should be on the cover letter, which they will take with them) if they have any questions or concerns at the conclusion of the study. There is a model for this on the pages that follow.

Information Typically Required in an IRB Protocol

PURPOSE: This section should be like a mini version of the Introduction to your paper. It should be between **10–20 sentences long**. You need to thoroughly describe *why* you are doing the study. Define and discuss the key concepts of your study (assuming your reader is not a social psychologist and has never read any of the articles that you are basing your study on); past research that has been conducted in the area (be sure to cite past research here); and why your study is necessary to conduct. Clearly explain what your specific hypotheses are, and what you hope that your results will show. The IRB uses this section to determine whether the benefits of the study outweigh the risks, so you need to be sure to convey *why* it is important!

- This information can be drawn from your assigned hypothesis in lab #10, your "rationale for your method selected" homework from lab #15, and the Introduction section from your paper drafts so far.

Research Methods and Procedures of the Study. This should also be about 10–20 sentences, depending on how complicated your procedures are. What research method are you using? What will participants do when they are in your study (provide a very detailed, step-by-step description). Although you will later describe recruitment and consent procedures, you need to state here—briefly—how you will get participants; where they will go to take part in the study; how much time will be required of them; when consent will take place; as well as when and how people will be debriefed. Refer the

IRB to supporting documents you will attach to the research protocol (cover letters, surveys, etc.). The IRB needs to fully understand here how you are testing the hypotheses that you described in the previous section.

- This information will be used again later, when you create your experimental protocols in lab # 19.

Variables. What are your independent and dependent variables?

- Get this from the measurement worksheet assigned during lab #16.

Describe equipment. If you are collecting data via a computer or some other method, state that. You do not need to list paper-pencil surveys. *If you are doing a paper-pencil survey, just state that no equipment will be used in the study.*

How will confidentiality or anonymity be maintained? Typically, you will assign participants a random identification number, and that will be the only way to identify them as participants. This ensures that participants will remain anonymous. If participants can be identified somehow (e.g., because you collected names or other personally identifying information), then this creates a risk for breach of confidentiality. You need to explain how this will be protected. If you are collecting data online, be sure to describe how no e-mail or IP addresses will be gathered (or if they are collected, why they are necessary and how you will keep this information confidential), and how data will be encrypted.

Describe how consent will be obtained. For the most part, you will probably be using cover letters, or possibly waivers (if you are conducting an observational design), in your project, so you need to describe when you will have participants read them; how you will address questions; etc. If a waiver of consent is used, a clear justification must be provided (see your instructor for this information).

How will research records be maintained during and after the project? You need to describe here how you will maintain them, during and after the study. If you are collecting data via computer, state "data will be stored on password-protected computers in a locked laboratory until the end of the semester, at which point the data will be deleted." If you are collecting data via paper-and-pencil surveys, state "no names or other identifying information will be collected about participants, and all surveys will be placed into a box or manila envelope by the participant. These surveys will not be examined until they have all been collected." If you are running a study where other participants or confederates are present, you need to have a statement for how you will deal with the fact that the participant may be recognized after the experiment by the confederate or other participant. How will you maintain their confidentiality then? By law, all real research records need to be maintained for a minimum of three years after the study, but because this is for educational purposes, all of your research protocols should contain the statement *"All data and materials collected for this project will be deleted or destroyed at the end of the semester in which data were obtained."*

How will the study be monitored? Describe here how your research team plans to ensure that you are following procedures and protocols. Specify that your instructor will monitor your progress through weekly meetings.

Subject Selection

How will subjects be recruited? Be very specific! It is vital that you are clear about not only where you will be recruiting, but when, and by whom. If you are using classrooms, do you have instructor permission? How will your recruitment statement be presented?

Characteristics of population. Be specific. Provide details on age, gender, etc., of your anticipated participants.

Number of participants. Try to be realistic. The total number depends on where you are doing the study; how you are recruiting them; etc. Many small projects like these have about 20 to 40 participants, but this will vary (for instance, if you are conducting an on-line study, you may have an easy time reaching a much higher number). Remember that you cannot collect data from more participants than you receive approval for, so request a number a little higher than you expect.

Inclusion/exclusion criteria. Be specific about any group of people you are including or excluding, and give reasons why. **Simply being under the age of 18 is not a good reason to exclude minors.** Typically, minors can participate in psychological research, but they must receive parental consent first. If you are surveying college students, and someone is under the age of 18, you need to provide sufficient justification as to why you would exclude them (for example, if you are studying voting intentions, you could make a compelling case for excluding minors because they are not legally able to vote). Alternatively, you could make an argument that the survey items and questions pose low-to-minimal risk, so parental consent will be waived for your study. You should specify, however, why they are low risk. Are the materials something that people would be exposed to on an everyday basis already?

Compensation. Depending on how and who you are sampling, participants may get extra credit. State here: "Participants will participate on a voluntary basis." If there is a possibility that they could get course credit, add the statement, "If the instructor allows, participants may be eligible for extra credit for participating in this research project. If, for any reason, the participant decides not to participate in this study, the instructor will provide alternatives for obtaining extra credit." If you have a specific class in mind, and know whether the students will get extra credit, you should include that information in the research protocol and consent form.

Criteria for exclusion. Be specific here regarding whether—and why—you might exclude certain participants. Generally speaking, there probably will not be many reasons for exclusion. Please note that this pertains to exclusion DURING the study, not afterward.

Risks and Discomforts

Describe any potential risks to subjects, and assess the likelihood and seriousness of these risks. You need to write something here, even if there are minimal risks. For instance, people may feel uncomfortable or embarrassed answering certain questions. There is ALWAYS some risk—no matter what method you use! If it is minimal, then state that it is so, and that the manipulation or method of inquiry that you are using has been demonstrated to have minimal effects in the past. You should cite past research to support this, if it is the case.

Describe ways to minimize risks. Even if there is very little risk for participants, you need to write something here. Be sure to state that participants will be reminded that they can stop partaking of the study at any time, and do not have to answer questions they are uncomfortable answering. You may also state that the experimenters may end the experiment if they feel that the participant is being harmed. If you are debriefing participants, this is a way to minimize risks, as well. Succinctly describe how they will be debriefed again.

If the methods create potential risks, describe other methods that were considered, and why they weren't used. You need to outline here WHY you are using the method that you are using, and why you decided to use it over other methods. Why a survey? What other methods did you consider during this class? Did using surveys minimize risk more than the others? How? Why

not use an observational method? Small group research? You may also want to explain how the method you chose has been used effectively in the past, with minimal negative impact. CITE those studies, to lend support to your choice in method!

- Pull this information from the "operationalization" worksheets that you completed for each of the methods we covered so far. You do not need to discuss all of them, but select at least two to compare.

Address procedures for maintaining confidentiality if a breach represents a risk. If all of your participants are anonymous, you need to explain this here. Anonymity would provide the least amount of risk. If they are not anonymous, you must specify how you will maintain their confidentiality.

Adverse events: You will need to state here how you will handle any adverse events that may arise while you are conducting your study.

Benefits: Receiving extra credit does not count here as a benefit. There may be no known benefits to the participants. You need to explain that here, and that the results of the study will enhance our knowledge of the topic that you are studying. **Give some detail** about what specifically your study will add to our empirical understanding of the topic. This is used to justify why, if there are any potential risks, your experiment or study is worth it. This section will be used to really determine whether the benefits outweigh any possible risks, so talk up what the implications to your findings would be to science, or to our understanding of human behavior. Be specific!

Cover Letter

[Sample cover letter]

[You are encouraged to model your cover letter after this one. If you choose not to use this format, your cover letter must include, at a minimum, the same elements as this model and the required texts. Before using this model, remove all italicized text. This may fit on one or two pages. If you are administering this cover letter online, change the wording appropriately.]

Dear Participant,

You are invited to take part in a project titled *[title]*, conducted as part of a class requirement for a social psychology laboratory at *[name of college or university]*. The research is being conducted by a group of students, *[names]*, enrolled in the class under the supervision of *[insert instructor's name]*. The purpose of this study is to *[Describe, at a 6th–8th grade reading level, why you are doing this study: What question do you hope to answer?]*. You are being asked to participate in this study because *[state here why they are being recruited, and why this person might qualify for the research study. What is it about them that makes them of interest to the research team? Also state reasons a participant could be excluded from volunteering, such as being a smoker, being under 18 years of age, being pregnant, etc.]*.

If you choose to take part in the project, you will *[Describe, at a 6th–8th grade reading level, the procedures of the study. This should provide adequate detail regarding what an individual can expect, so that there are no "surprises." Be sure to state where the project will take place.]*. Your participation will require approximately _____ minutes of your time. *[If applicable, describe in lay terms any reason a participant might be removed from the study: e.g., "If you fail to show up to all sessions, you may be removed from the study."]*

[Describe possible risks here. If there are no known risks associated with the procedures/treatment, include a statement to that effect.] It is not possible to identify all potential risks in research procedures, but the researcher(s) have taken reasonable safeguards to minimize any known and potential, but unknown, risks.

The information collected in the study will be used for educational purposes only, and will not be published or presented at professional meetings. Your information will be combined with information from other people taking part in the study. You will not be identified in these materials. *[IF THE STUDY IS ANONYMOUS: state, "This study is anonymous. That means that no one, not even members of the research team, will know that the information you give comes from you."]* The information you submit will *[State here how you will keep their responses anonymous or confidential, as well as how the data will be stored.]*. All data and records from this project will be deleted or destroyed at the end of the current semester.

Your participation is completely voluntary. [*If participants can get extra credit, insert this statement: "If your instructor allows, you may be eligible for extra credit for participating in this research project. If, for any reason, you would not like to participate, your instructor should also offer an alternative for obtaining extra credit."*] If you decide to participate in the study, you may withdraw your consent and stop participating at any time, without penalty or loss of benefits to which you are otherwise entitled. Before you decide whether to accept this invitation to take part in the study, please ask any questions that might come to mind now. Later, if you have questions about the study, you can contact the supervising instructor(s): [*Insert instructor's name and contact information.*] We will give you a copy of this cover letter to take with you.

Debriefing Information

[MODEL DEBRIEFING FORM]

[You are encouraged to model your debriefing after this one. If you choose not to use this format, your debriefing must include, at a minimum, the same elements as this model and the required texts. Before using this model, remove all italicized text. This will most likely fit on one or two pages.]

Project Title:

[Title]

Investigators:

[Instructor's name here]
Primary Investigator
Phone: *[phone #]*
Office: *[office #]*
E-mail: *[address]*

[Your names here]
Co-Investigators
Phone: *[phone #]*
Office: *[office #]*
E-mail: *[address]*

Purpose of the Study:

This is a research study about *[Insert detailed information here, in simple terms about the purpose of the study.]*. We are specifically interested in *[Describe your hypotheses in simple terms.]*. The results of this study will help us to understand *[Briefly describe the importance of your study, and what it will hopefully add, or the potential significance of the work. Describe your hypotheses, in an easily understandably way. This section should thoroughly explain to the participants—in simple terms—the true purpose of the study, and educate them about your topic.]*.

Methods/Procedures:

As a participant in this study, you were asked to *[Insert information about what they specifically did in the study, and why that particular method was used. This should be very detailed, and explain all experimental conditions.]*.

Use of the Data:

All the responses you gave in this study are confidential, and cannot be traced to you in any way. Your information will be combined with information from other people taking part in the study, and your individual answers will not be taken into account unless combined with other people's answers. When we write about the study to share it with other researchers, we will write about the combined information we have gathered. You will not be identified in these written materials.

Implications and Applications:

While there are no direct benefits from participation in this study, your participation will help us to understand *[Say a lot here. Tell them all about how their results will add to what we know about the topic, and what scientific and societal implications there might be. This should make them feel good about participating and happy that they contributed to science.]*.

We would like to thank you for participating in this study. If you are interested in learning about the results of this study once the data have been collected, analyzed, and interpreted, please notify the researchers. Because we are currently running this study with more people, we also ask that you do not tell others about the specific content of the study, because they may answer questions differently based on this knowledge.

Lab #18

Purpose:

- The purpose of this lab is to allow time for groups to finish completing their IRB materials for mock review.

Objectives:

- Work with research team to get materials completed for IRB approval. These are due by the end of class time.

Homework:

- None!

EXPERIMENTAL
PROTOCOLS

Lab #19

Purpose:

- The purpose of this lab is to revise IRB documents in class, and develop experimental protocols.

Objectives:

- Make revisions to IRB documents.
- Review the following section entitled Developing an Experimental Protocol as well as the sample that follows and create an experimental protocol for your own study.

Homework:

- Submit final IRB revisions to your lab instructor.
- Experimental protocol.

Developing an Experimental Protocol

Now that you have tentative mock IRB approval to proceed with your study, you need to develop an experimental protocol to conduct the work. This protocol is sort of a step-by-step procedure guide that can be given to almost any research assistant to follow. By having a protocol, researchers ensure that the administration of their study is standardized, and that participants are all treated similarly.

Your task for the lab today is to develop a protocol for your study. Because each study and method is so different, your lab group's protocol will look very different from someone else's. But, the final product should be a one-to-three-page "manual," with specific steps for a researcher to follow in conducting your specific study. It may contain specific phrases that are read to each participant; randomization instructions; information about how data files are accessed/saved; etc. This should be a VERY specific document.

Have this protocol ready for the next lab.

Example of an Experimental Protocol: Myspace Study

(used with permmission from Jennifer J. Harman, Ph.D.)

Prior to start of study:

1. Get: Protocol binder, consent forms, study sign, and debriefing forms (on the floor immediately to your right in C-79—the room with the computers).
2. Put study sign on door (study #3)
3. Log on to the computers in C-79 that will be used for data collection.
4. Open MediaLab on each computer (click icon on desktop).
   a. Select "Run" on top left corner.
   b. Select "Run an experiment."
   c. This should open up the T drive (if not, you need to open up the T drive first, before accessing the file).
   d. Open the MediaLab Study folder.
   e. Open "Risk Perception Study" folder.
   f. You should find a file named "Risk Perception Phase 3."
   g. Open this file.
   h. Type in their participant number (refer to participant ID section of this binder). Check off participant numbers as you use them.
      i. Note: There are separate sheets for men and women in the binder for this.
   i. For condition: Type in condition # (next to participant # on participant ID sheet).
      i. *It is important that you type in the correct participant ID and matching condition.*
5. Place two copies of the consent form for each participant on the keyboards of the computers that will be used for data collection.

Data Collection:

1. As participants arrive, tell them which computer to sit in front of, and ask them to read the consent form.
2. Wait until a few minutes after the scheduled start time of the study to begin.
   a. If a participant arrives after this time, allow them to participate in the study as long as there is enough time remaining for them to finish.
3. When all participants have arrived, put sign on door saying "Do not disturb: Study in progress."
   a. Ask participants' names and take attendance
4. Go over the consent form with participants. Have participants initial the bottom of each page, and sign the last page. You must also sign the last page. You must complete two copies of the consent form for each participant.
   a. Keep one copy of the consent form for our records.
   b. Let participant know they need to keep the second consent form as proof of their participation in the study.
5. Tell them to read instructions that are presented to them carefully, to raise their hand if they have any questions during the study, and to let you know when they have completed the survey.
6. Give participants a copy of the debriefing form, go over it in detail with them, answer questions, and thank them for their time.
7. When you have finished data collection for the day, make sure to:
   a. Take the study sign down from the door.
   b. Return study sign, protocol binder, and any unused consent/debriefing forms to where you found them.
   c. Log off all computers.
   d. Turn off lights and lock door before you leave.

DATA ANALYSIS AND STATISTICS

Lab #20

Purpose:

- The purpose of this lab is to provide an introduction to basic statistics used in the analysis phase of social psychological research.

Objectives:

- Review and discuss the following section entitled Data Analysis and Statistics.
- Learn about descriptive and inferential statistics.
- Learn about measures of central tendency, correlations, t-tests, and ANOVAs.
- Learn about different statistical packages and interpret output.
- Practice using a statistical package.

Homework:

- Study for quiz on labs #16–20.

Data Analysis and Statistics

THE unfortunate reality is that analyzing data is not a simple and straightforward process, and before you can even begin thinking of running your analyses, you will need to do a bit of work to get your data into shape first. In this section, we will focus on how to prepare quantitative data for analysis.

Preparing to Analyze Data

Once you have your data, the first thing you will need to do is "clean" it. This does not mean scrubbing your surveys or wiping down your computer screen; but rather, ensuring that the values in your data set are correct, or conform to a set of rules. For example, if you have a nominal variable in your dataset such as gender with values coded as 1 = *male*, 2 = *female*, and 3 = *transgendered*, then you would not want to see any numbers other than 1, 2, or 3 listed under that variable. Errors can be introduced when survey data are typed in manually, and occasionally values can be mislabeled in computerized data sets. One way to diagnose this problem is to perform frequency counts on the values for each variable. If you see some values that should not be there, then you need to go back to your dataset to find the mistakes and correct them.

Another step some of you may have to take in preparing your data is creating "dummy codes," or nominal distinctions chosen by you to indicate different levels of certain variables (e.g., independent variable conditions, gender, race, sexual orientation, etc.). If you use an online survey program to collect your data, dummy codes are usually assigned automatically; however, if you are entering data from a pencil-and-paper survey by hand, you will need to come up with these yourself.

Next, you will need to reverse-code any con-trait items in order to compute your composite variables. For example, let us say that you assessed self-esteem with two items rated on a 5-point scale (where 1 = *strongly disagree* and 5 = *strongly agree*): "I feel very positively about myself" and "I feel worthless." Before you could create your self-esteem composite variable that averages across scores on these two items, you would need to reverse-code participants' scores on the latter item so that higher scores on each item correspond with higher levels of self-esteem. The easiest way to do this is to take the maximum value on your scale (in this case, 5), add 1 to it, and then subtract each observation from this number. So, in our self-esteem example, we would subtract each observation from 6. This means that if a participant gave a response of 1 (*strongly disagree*) to the item "I feel worthless," their score would be a 5 after reverse-coding it. Do not average across any variables until you have done any necessary reverse-coding first, otherwise your statistical analyses will be thrown way off.

Next, you may want to look for **outliers**, or data points that are far beyond what you might expect for a given variable. For Likert-type response scales (e.g., the 5-point scale mentioned above for assessing self-esteem), you do not really need to worry about outliers because there is such a restricted range of responses to start with. However, for items in which participants are asked to generate their own value (e.g., annual income, number of lifetime sexual partners), outliers are a potential concern because averages are subject to distortion by extreme responses. For example, if you were to ask 100 people about their annual income, but you happened to have one or two billionaires in your sample, they would artificially inflate the average, which could throw off any statistical comparisons you wanted to make. There are many ways to handle outliers, but you will want to discuss with your instructor the best way to detect and deal with them. Keep in mind that if you delete any outliers, you must be upfront about this and be able to justify why in your reporting of the results.

Along the same lines, you will also want to check that your data meet the assumptions for the statistical tests you plan to employ. Most of the analyses you might use in this class (e.g., ANOVA and linear regression) assume that data have a normal distribution curve, that all data points are independent of one another, and that the variables have linear relationships. Therefore, you will want to check for potential **skewness** (i.e., are the majority of observations for a given variable clustered at the extreme ends of the scale?) and **kurtosis** (i.e., is the distribution of values for a given variable flat instead of shaped like a bell curve?). You will also want to ensure that the variables that you are considering have a linear relationship with one other (e.g., by checking scatterplots of the data). If these assumptions are not met, then you may need to consider either transforming your data (e.g., log transformations), or use a different statistical analysis that

allows for non-normal data. You should discuss strategies for testing these assumptions and potential remedies with your instructor because there are many different ways of handling this.

It is also a good idea to check and see whether the measures you administered have an acceptable level of reliability by computing Cronbach's alpha, a test of internal consistency. All major statistical programs can compute this; however, you need to make sure to do any reverse-coding necessary before calculating this number. Generally speaking, a reliability coefficient of at least .70 is considered the bare minimum for acceptability; however, it is preferable to have numbers in the range of .80 or .90. If you are using a measure that someone else created, you should ensure that your reliability coefficient is comparable to the numbers that appear in other published reports. Demonstrating high levels of reliability for your measures is important because it enhances your study's internal validity (i.e., your confidence that the independent variable is responsible for the observed changes in the dependent variable). If your measures are not reliable, it is difficult to conclude cause-and-effect in an experimental design.

Data Analysis

After your data have been cleaned, your composite variables created, and your assumptions checked, you can start your analyses! This is the exciting part. To determine the appropriate analysis, you will first need to decide whether your outcome variable is continuous (e.g., a ratio scale, such as income or age) or categorical (e.g., a nominal scale, such as gender or racial categories). If you have a continuous outcome, your analytic options would include t-tests and ANOVA (for testing differences between groups), or correlation and regression (for testing the strength of the association between variables). If your outcome is categorical, you would need to consider other strategies, such as Chi-square or logistic regression. You should discuss with your instructor the type of analysis that would best suit the data you are working with.

Before conducting hypothesis tests, most researchers start by gathering some basic descriptive information about their sample. Typically, this includes describing the age of your participants (mean, standard deviation, and range), the proportion of your sample comprising each gender and racial group, and any other relevant demographic characteristics you assessed (e.g., relationship status, education level). In addition, researchers usually compute and present means and standard deviations of all independent and dependent variables used in their analyses. Occasionally, researchers also present a correlation table to demonstrate how all of their study's variables were associated, even if correlation is not how they plan to test their hypotheses

On the following page, we present a brief summary of different statistical analyses that you might use for your projects. This is by no means an exhaustive list of the different approaches that could be used, but these are most often used by students taking this course.

Statistics Summary Page

BELOW is a quick summary of some of the most basic statistics that you may use to analyze your data. You should work with your instructor to determine which analysis will make the most sense to use for your project.

Abbreviation	Statistic	What is it?
R, *r*, or Pearson's R	Correlation	A measure of the strength of the linear relationship between two variables.
t	T-test	Assesses whether the means of **two** groups or samples are *statistically* different from one another.
ANOVA	Analysis of Variance	A statistical test of whether the means of **several** groups are all equal to or different from each other (generalizes the *t*-test to more than two groups).
B or β (standardized)	Regression	Estimates the average value of the dependent variable (usually denoted by y). when the independent variable(s) (usually denoted by x) is held fixed.
χ^2	Chi-square	Investigates whether distributions of categorical variables differ from one another. Compares the tallies or counts of categorical responses between two (or more) independent groups.

Statistical Programs

In order to analyze the data that you collect, you will need access to a statistical program. There are a number of different options you could potentially use, but the specific program you will use for this course will depend upon which license(s) your University maintains. The most commonly used statistical programs by social psychologists include:

- SPSS (http://www.spss.com/)
- SAS (http://www.sas.com/)
- R (http://www.r-project.org/)

All of these programs have different capabilities, and some are more powerful than others. However, for purposes of this course, any of these programs would work, because you will be conducting relatively basic statistical procedures. We have included links for each program above, because many of them offer free trials. Also, in the event that your university does not have statistical programs available to students, please note that R is a completely free program that you could even download on your home computer.

DATA COLLECTION

Lab #21

Purpose:

- The purpose of this lab is to conduct a mock run-through of your experiment or study.

Objectives:

- Take quiz on labs #16–20.
- Practice running the study with classmates, using experimental protocols.
- Make modifications to protocol as needed.

Homework:

- None!

Lab #22

Purpose:

- Begin collecting data.

Objectives:

- Gain experience obtaining consent from participants, collecting and saving data, and debriefing.

Homework:

- Revision of Introduction and Method sections.

Lab #23

Purpose:

- Finish collecting data.

Objectives:

- Gain experience obtaining consent from participants, collecting and saving data, and debriefing.

Homework:

- Finish collecting data.

Lab #24

Purpose:

- Finish any remaining data collection and begin constructing data sets.

Objectives:

- Learn how to set up data files.
- Enter data in class and score surveys, if needed.

Homework:

- Have all data entered and scored into a statistical program.

Constructing Data Sets for Analysis

DEPENDING upon what statistical program you are using to analyze your data, you may need to set up your file differently. There are a number of great Web resources available to help you decide how to set up your file.

Generally speaking, you want to have a unique entry for each variable you measure, for each participant. Each program has different ways of labeling your data, entering values, etc. Become familiar with the recommended steps for the analysis program you are using before you start entering your data.

Use labels for your variables that are intuitive, descriptive, and easy to understand. For example, if you use a validated scale such as the Beck Depression Inventory (BDI) in your study, maybe label the items from this questionnaire as BDI1, BDI2, BDI3—and so on. This is much easier to interpret later in your analyses than if you just assign sequential numbers to your questionnaire items that do not have any meaning (e.g., variable1, variable2, variable3).

Excel

(Please note that most statistical programs can read data from Excel files. If you already have some familiarity with Excel, you may find this to be the easiest program to work with for data entry.)

http://www.stanford.edu/group/ssds/cgi-bin/drupal/files/Guides/Using%20Excel.pdf

SPSS

http://www.stattutorials.com/SPSS/TUTORIAL-SPSS-Create-a-data-set.htm

SAS

http://www.umass.edu/statdata/software/handouts/sas_on-line/enteringdata.html

R

http://cran.r-project.org/doc/manuals/R-data.html

DATA INTERPRETATION, WRITING, AND DISSEMINATION

Data Interpretation

Now that you are finished collecting your data, it is time for the exciting part—seeing what you found! During the next few labs, we will focus on putting datasets together, performing analyses, and writing about the results in APA Style.

For students who are relatively new to statistics, analyzing and interpreting your data may appear to be a daunting task. To assist with this, we provide links to helpful online resources that can walk you through virtually any type of analytic procedure you might need using the statistical program of your choice. We also provide some sample exercises to help you practice writing about statistics in APA style before writing up your own findings in your final paper.

Before you begin your analyses, it is important to keep in mind that you may not find what you are looking for. If your predictions are not supported, this does not mean that you failed, and it does not necessarily mean that your predictions were incorrect. Every social psychologist conducts at least some studies that do not work out, and this may occur for any number of reasons. Of course, sometimes our predictions are simply wrong. Other times, we discover a confounding variable that we failed to account for. Yet other times, a null result may be due to a lack of **statistical power**—in other words, perhaps not enough participants were recruited to detect an effect. Lack of power is an issue that frequently occurs in student research because limited resources and time constraints make it challenging to recruit large enough samples to detect differences between your experimental and comparison groups.

In short, please do not be too discouraged if your hypotheses are not supported. This is an experience that all researchers have had at one time or another and it is an inevitable part of being a psychological scientist.

Lab #25

Purpose:

- The purpose of this lab is to analyze your study's results in class with your instructor.

Objectives:

- Practice analyzing data using a statistical package.
- Print up output of analyses.

Homework:

- Bring output to next class.

Running Your Analyses

F ORTUNATELY, there are many resources online to help walk you through running your analyses, no matter which statistical program you use. The tutorials also typically describe how to read the output. Below are just a few examples, but doing a basic search with Google—or any other search engine—can pull up a number of other resources for you.

SPSS

ANOVAs
http://academic.udayton.edu/gregelvers/
psy216/SPSS/1wayanova.htm
bama.ua.edu/~jhartman/689/facanova.ppt

Regression
http://academic.udayton.edu/gregelvers/
psy216/SPSS/reg.htm

Chi-Square
http://www.stanford.edu/group/ssds/cgi-bin/
drupal/files/Guides/Using%20Excel.pdf

SAS

Syntax for a number of different analyses
http://www.ats.ucla.edu/stat/sas/whatstat/
whatstat.htm

ANOVAs
http://support.sas.com/documentation/
cdl/en/statug/63033/HTML/default/viewer.
htm#anova_toc.htm

Regression
http://www.ats.ucla.edu/stat/sas/webbooks/
reg/

Chi-Square
http://support.sas.com/documentation/
cdl/en/procstat/63104/HTML/default/viewer.
htm#procstat_freq_sect029.htm

R

ANOVAs
http://www.personality-project.org/R/r.
anova.html
http://www.statmethods.net/stats/anova.html

Regression
http://www.jeremymiles.co.uk/
regressionbook/extras/appendix2/R/

Chi-Square
http://www.cyclismo.org/tutorial/R/
probability.html

Excel

ANOVAs
http://org.elon.edu/econ/sac/anova.htm

Regression
http://www.jeremymiles.co.uk/
regressionbook/extras/appendix2/excel/

Chi-Square
http://www.gifted.uconn.edu/siegle/research/
ChiSquare/chiexcel.htm
http://org.elon.edu/econ/sac/chisquare.htm

Lab #26

Purpose:

- Learn how to interpret data and write Results sections.
- Learn how to present data graphically.

Objectives:

- Go over output from statistical analysis.
- Decide whether to use a figure, graph, or table for your paper, and learn how to create them.
- Complete in-class output writing exercise.
- Learn how to write the Results section using APA formatting.

Homework:

- Draft of Results section.

Putting Your Statistical Output into Words

WrITING up the results of your analyses can be tricky. The following pages include sample output from several analyses. Work with your group to put the results into words. Write two to three sentences explaining each analysis. Reference your APA manual to see how to correctly report this information.

(*Please note: All data output that appears below is from SPSS.*)

1. A research team examined whether there were significant differences on an intimacy scale between men and women. They ran a T-Test and got the following results.

Group Statistics

	What is your gender?	N	Mean	Std. Deviation	Std. Error Mean
Intimacy Score	Male	61	3.6512	.47964	.06141
	Female	87	3.8825	.49787	.05338

Independent Samples Test

		Levene's Test for Equality of Variances		t-test for Equality of Means					95% Confidence Interval of the Difference	
		F	Sig.	t	df	Sig. (2-tailed)	Mean Difference	Std. Error Difference	Lower	Upper
Intimacy Score	Equal variances assumed	.125	.724	-2.824	146	.005	-.23132	.08191	-.39319	-.06945
	Equal variances not assumed			-2.843	132.243	.005	-.23132	.08137	-.39227	-.07037

In the space below, please write two to three sentences describing the results of this analysis.

2. A research team was interested in whether depression was related to feelings of trust and intimacy for men who are in relationships. They conducted a correlational analysis, and these were their results:

Correlations

		Depression	Emotional Intimacy	Trust
Depression	Pearson Correlation	1	-.430**	-.375**
	Sig. (2-tailed)		.001	.004
	N	56	56	56
Emotional Intimacy	Pearson Correlation	-.430**	1	.687**
	Sig. (2-tailed)	.001		.000
	N	56	56	56
Trust	Pearson Correlation	-.375**	.687**	1
	Sig. (2-tailed)	.004	.000	
	N	56	56	56

** Correlation is significant at the 0.01 level (2-tailed).

In the space below, please write two or three sentences describing the results of this analysis.

3. A research group collected survey data to see whether self-esteem would predict the amount of alcohol their participants drank during the past week. Alcohol use was scored on a 4-point scale, ranging from 1 = Never; 2 = 1 time per week; 3 = 2 times per week; and 4 = 3 or more times per week. The self-esteem scale was scored such that higher values indicated higher levels of self-esteem. They ran a regression analysis, and got the following results.

Model Summary

Model	R	R Square	Adjusted R Square	Std. Error of the Estimate
1	.186[a]	.034	.026	1.021

a. Predictors: (Constant), Self-EsteemScale

ANOVA[b]

Model		Sum of Squares	df	Mean Square	F	Sig.
1	Regression	4.163	1	4.163	3.994	.048[a]
	Residual	116.758	112	1.042		
	Total	120.921	113			

a. Predictors: (Constant), SelfEsteemScale

b. Dependent Variable: On average, how often did you drink alcohol over the past week?

Coefficients[a]

Model		Unstandardized Coefficients		Standardized Coefficients	t	Sig.
		B	Std. Error	Beta		
1	(Constant)	.718	.635		1.130	.261
	Self-EsteemScale	.040	.020	.186	1.998	.048

a. Dependent Variable: On average, how often did you drink alcohol over the past week?

In the space below, please write two to three sentences describing this result.

4. A research group conducted an experiment, in which they had half of their participants write about what it would be like to die (mortality salience condition), and the other half wrote about dental pain. They were interested in seeing whether this impacted the appeal of taking physical risks (e.g., sky diving). They were also interested in seeing whether there would be gender differences. They ran a univariate ANOVA, and got the following results.

Between-Subjects Factors

		Value Label	N
Experimental Condition	.00	Dental	84
	1.00	Death	75
Gender	.00	Male	65
	1.00	Female	94

Tests of Between-Subjects Effects

Dependent Variable: Risk Appeal

Source	Type III Sum of Squares	df	Mean Square	F	Sig.
Corrected Model	34.893[a]	3	11.631	9.266	.000
Intercept	3397.127	1	3397.127	2706.419	.000
Condition	.431	1	.431	.343	.559
Sex	33.846	1	33.846	26.965	.000
Condition * Sex	1.450	1	1.450	1.155	.284
Error	194.558	155	1.255		
Total	3624.917	159			
Corrected Total	229.450	158			

a. R Squared = .152 (Adjusted R Squared = .136)

In the space below, please write two to three sentences describing this result.

Draft of Results Section

For the next lab, you will turn in the Results section of your paper after conducting the analyses of your experiment. Be sure to follow APA formatting in reporting your findings. Also, submit any changes you have made to all of your other sections. Your paper should be starting to come together, and look more polished. Be sure to include any edits/comments that your instructor gave you from the last paper. When you turn in your Results section, be sure to also turn in a copy of your data output from the statistical program you used. This will help your instructor give you feedback on your draft.

You are also required to present one table, graph, or figure in your paper (examples are included on the next page). These can be somewhat difficult to do while complying with APA formatting, so we suggest turning them in this week, rather than waiting until the final draft of your paper. You will want the feedback.

Writing a Results Section

The Results section should not be particularly difficult to write, because the main thing you do here is present the statistical findings from your study. If you are new to statistics, though, you may find this to be a bit more challenging. This section will probably be relatively short, unless you have a lot of hypotheses. The format is a little flexible, but most sections will start by reminding the reader of the hypothesis, stating whether or not it was supported, and then presenting the results of the relevant hypothesis test.

Below are some tips for writing a good Results section:

- Do not just throw numbers at the reader: Explain what they mean. For example, after reporting a correlation coefficient, state what that number indicates (i.e., "the correlation between X and Y was .35, meaning that as variable X increases, so does variable Y").
- Do not spend too much time interpreting the results, or speculating on why your hypothesis was not supported. That is what the Discussion section is for.
- You should state what statistical technique you used to test your hypothesis (e.g., *t*-test, chi-square, correlation, etc.), but you do not need to explain how this technique works. You can assume most readers will already have some knowledge of statistics.

For additional information on writing a Results section, please consult the APA Publication Manual. You may also find the following websites helpful:

- http://owl.english.purdue.edu/owl/resource/670/04/
- http://web.psych.washington.edu/writingcenter/writingguides/pdf/stats.pdf

Sample Figure and Table

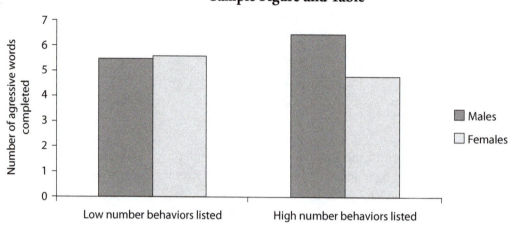

Figure 1. Aggressive words listed as a function of jealous behaviors and gender

Table 1

Summary of Regression Analysis for Texting Frequency and Attributions on Anxiety and Relationship Similarity (N = 134)

Variable	B	SE B	β
Anxiety			
Step 1			
Frequency of texting	-.89	.56	-.28
Step 2			
Frequency of texting	-.77	.50	-.18
Attributions about texting	4.63	1.88	.21*
Similarity			
Step 1			
Frequency of texting	.20	.09	.29**
Step 2			
Frequency of texting	.25	.10	.34**
Attributions about texting	-.42	.31	-.17

Note: Anxiety R^2= .03 for Step 1; ΔR^2 = .09 for Step 2 (p =.01). Similarity R^2= .10 for Step 1; ΔR^2 = .03 for Step 2 (p= .18). *p < .02. ** p < .01.

Lab #27

Purpose:

- Learn how to write the Discussion section and abstract of your paper.

Objectives:

- Learn how to write a Discussion section and an abstract.

Homework:

- Draft of Discussion section and abstract of your paper.

Draft of Discussion Section and Abstract

For the next lab, you will turn in the Discussion section and abstract of your paper. Be sure to follow APA formatting in reporting your results. Also, submit any changes you have made to all of your other sections. Your paper should start to look much more complete and polished. Be sure to include any edits/comments that your instructor gave you from the last paper.

Writing a Discussion Section

Students who are new to writing scientific research papers often find the Discussion section to be the most difficult part to write. One of the most common concerns we hear from students is that the findings are already clearly explained in the Results section, so a Discussion seems unnecessary and redundant. However, a good Discussion section does much more than just summarize the findings, and, in fact, is actually one of the most important parts of any scientific paper.

The Discussion section is valuable, because it gives the author a chance to interpret the findings and tell the reader what to make of them. You might be saying, "But don't the results explain themselves?" Not necessarily. For example, let's say that you conducted an experiment to study the link between temperature and aggressive behavior. In this study, you put participants in either a hot room or a cold room, and then give them a frustrating computer task to complete.

You hypothesized that participants in the hot room would be more likely to respond to the task with anger (e.g., by yelling at or hitting the computer). However, let's say that you found no difference in aggression between participants in the hot room and the cold room. If your paper simply ended after reporting these findings, people might walk away thinking that there is no link between temperature and aggression (when, in fact, they are very strongly related in reality). By including a Discussion section, you can explain why your study did not work as planned (e.g., maybe the temperature did not get hot enough; perhaps participants guessed the purpose of the study and controlled their anger; etc.) and situate your results in the context of the broader literature. This helps to ensure that people do not walk away from your paper with any misconceptions. It also helps to inform other researchers about things they might want to try or avoid in their own work. Thus, crafting a good Discussion section is very important, for a variety of reasons.

Discussion sections are highly variable from paper to paper, because there is no standard structure that applies to them. However, most Discussion sections will include some common elements. They tend to begin by addressing specific details of your study, moving to more general points about how your work ties into the broader field. Below is a summary of the kinds of things you should do in your paper's Discussion section:

- Provide a brief rundown of the results, and whether they supported the hypotheses.
- Acknowledge any odd or unexpected findings.
- Discuss the strengths and limitations of your work.
- Relate your findings to existing theories and/or other relevant studies.
- Address the theoretical and/or practical implications of your findings.
- Offer your general conclusions.

Writing an Abstract

Writing an effective abstract can also be challenging, because it requires you to try and convey your entire paper in a very small amount of space. It is important to do this well, however, because the abstract is the first—and sometimes only—part of your paper that other people will see. A well-written abstract will entice people to read the full paper, and this is ultimately what you want. Otherwise, why did you go to the trouble of writing this paper in the first place?

Most abstracts follow a pretty simple formula, and adhere to the same word limits (approximately 150 total words, give or take 50). The elements of a good abstract are as follows. Please note that only one or two sentences are used to address each point:

- *Statement of the problem or research question.* Tell the reader what you addressed in your research, and why this is an important area to study.
- *Your approach to the problem or research question.* Tell the reader how you went about addressing this issue. What method(s) did you use (e.g., survey, experiment), and what were the major variables included?
- *A summary of the results.* What did you find? Provide a brief summary of the major findings.
- *A conclusion statement.* What does it all mean? What are the implications of your study? Discuss the take-home message. If space permits, you can address some of the major theoretical or practical applications of your findings.

For additional information on writing an abstract and a Discussion section, please consult the APA Publication Manual. You may also find the following website helpful: http://owl.english.purdue.edu/owl/resource/670/04/

Lab #28

Purpose:

- The purpose of this lab is to learn how research findings in social psychology are disseminated, and how to give an oral presentation of experimental results.

Objectives:

- Review the following sections entitled Research Dissemination and Poster Presentations. Learn about various outlets for social psychology research (journal articles, conferences, etc.), and the value of sharing results with the scientific community.
- Learn about different forms of presentations given at scientific conferences (i.e., talks vs. posters)
- Students will learn techniques in giving an effective research presentation.
- Work collaboratively with your lab group to create and orally present your study using Power-Point.

Homework:

- Prepare your oral presentation.
- Complete Research Experience Journal.

Research Dissemination

You are finished collecting and analyzing your data—now what? Although you may have satisfied your own curiosity at this point, your work is not finished. Your findings have the potential to contribute to the existing body of literature, to help other psychologists build theories, and to inform policy decisions; however, if you do not share your results, none of this can happen. Some have even argued that it is unethical to have participants volunteer their time, but not disseminate the research findings in at least some form to a larger audience. The two most common ways that psychologists share their research findings are through publications in peer-reviewed journals and presentations at conferences.

Publishing in Peer-Reviewed Journals

The paper you are writing for this course mirrors the kind of papers social psychologists typically write about their own research projects. The only real difference is that social psychologists would go one step further and submit their paper to a peer-reviewed journal for publication consideration. Getting published in one of these journals can be challenging and may take a long time, but many of us see this as a small price to pay for the benefits provided by the peer-review process.

When a paper is submitted to a journal, the editor will send it out for review to a few experts, who will weigh in with their critiques and suggestions for improvement. This process helps to identify potential errors in logic and reasoning, incorrect statistical procedures and results, as well as oversights and omissions from the literature review. The goal is to help "weed out" those papers that do not make an important contribution or that suffer from fatal flaws, while also enhancing the quality of those papers that go on to be published.

When reviews are favorable and editors see potential in a paper, they will usually give authors a chance to revise and resubmit their work for further publication consideration (papers are almost never accepted immediately because some questions the author did not anticipate undoubtedly arise). A revision opportunity is not a guarantee of eventual acceptance of the paper by the journal; rather, it simply is a chance for the author to address the comments and questions that came up during the initial review. If the author can address them satisfactorily, the paper will likely proceed toward publication.

When a paper is fatally flawed (e.g., there is a major confounding variable) or when the findings are unoriginal (e.g., they have been demonstrated many times before using the same types of samples), rejection is the most likely outcome. However, this does not necessarily spell the end for the paper or for the author's career. Oftentimes, authors will use the feedback from the reviews to conduct follow-up studies that are even more powerful and important, resulting in a stronger paper. As you can see, peer review is designed both to ensure that the research that ends up in print is of the highest possible quality, and also to help make all of us better scientists.

Giving Conference Presentations

The publication process can be lengthy. The time it takes to conduct peer-review, prepare revisions, and potentially go through more peer-review and revisions can take months or even years. In addition, journals often have publication lags on top of that, which means that it can potentially be a year or longer before a paper that is finally accepted for publication sees the light of day. In order to cope with this reality and get findings out to other scientists and the public sooner, psychologists frequently deliver conference presentations. Conference presentations are where you will hear about the cutting-edge research. If you stay in this field long enough, you will quickly come to realize that what you see in print is old news.

The classic conference presentation is a 10–15 minute talk given by one person that covers a recent study (sometimes two). Like papers submitted for publication, conference talks also go through a peer-review process of sorts; however, the process is much shorter and authors do not receive formal feedback other than accept/reject. Authors will submit brief abstracts to a conference committee, who will evaluate the merits of the work and whether it appears to be theoretically and methodologically sound. If so, it will be placed on the conference program. The time from acceptance to presentation is just a few months, which allows for incredibly fast dissemination of new findings.

The talks usually mirror the format of a typical research paper (i.e., Introduction, Methods, Results, and Discussion); however, due to the limited amount of time speakers are given, the details are greatly condensed. Thus, it is important to choose your words carefully when giving a conference talk. At the end of such talks, the audience is usually given a chance to ask questions, so be prepared!

Helpful pointers on delivering an effective conference-style presentation are provided later in this book along with the instructions for giving your final in-class presentation.

Poster Presentations

An Alternative to the Research Talk

WHEN most students imagine a conference presentation, they visualize a person standing up and giving a talk in front of a large audience. However, this is not the only way that research findings are conveyed at psychology conferences. Another common format is to deliver a poster presentation. Posters contain the same information as a typical conference talk, except that all of the information is printed and displayed on a large board. To make the information easier to read, it is usually condensed only to the most important points. Additionally, visual depictions of data (i.e., tables and figures) are often used to convey the findings as clearly as possible.

Psychology conferences usually schedule several thematic poster sessions in which a few dozen or perhaps a few hundred posters on a given topic (e.g., close relationships, stereotyping and prejudice) will be hung in a designated area for a specified period of time (usually one or two hours). The authors will stand by their own posters while attendees wander around the room, stopping to read those posters that sound interesting or catch their eye. The author is then available to answer questions or provide additional details. Authors usually bring handouts with them that summarize the research and provide their contact information in case any conference attendees want to learn more about the research or cite it.

Poster presentations allow you to have a very fast and informal exchange of ideas with many people in a short period of time, which makes it very different from the typical conference talk. As a result, some people prefer to give poster presentations because they enjoy the interaction and find the format to be less stressful. It is also an excellent opportunity to network and discuss ideas with people who share similar interests.

Creating a Poster

Most posters are created as a single slide in PowerPoint (or a similar computer program) and then printed out on a poster printer (if your department does not own one of these, posters can be printed at any local copy shop, although they are not cheap if you have to pay for it on your own). The standard sections included in a poster are typically: Introduction, Methods, Results, Discussion, and References. Including an abstract is optional.

A sample conference poster appears on the following page; however, please be aware that poster format varies considerably. You may opt to include less text, more tables and figures, photos of your stimuli, and so forth. Posters can also be personalized in terms of color scheme and font; however, the key to a successful poster is to make it readable from a distance and professional looking.

For additional pointers on creating conference posters and sample poster templates, see:

- http://colinpurrington.com/tips/academic/posterdesign
- http://www.youtube.com/watch?v= MqgjgwIXadA
- http://www.rcjournal.com/contents/10.04/ 10.04.1213.pdf

Social Influence and Attraction to Interracial Romantic Relationships

Justin J. Lehmiller   William G. Graziano

Purdue University

Abstract

In this experiment, White, heterosexual participants rated their physical attraction to several prospective targets of the other sex (some Black, some White). Prior to rating each target, participants were given artificial social comparison information (positive, negative, or none) from supposed peers. Results indicated that participants' attraction to the targets was significantly affected by whether they believed their peers found the target to be attractive or unattractive. This effect held for both same and different race targets.

Introduction

One factor that affects interpersonal attraction is social influence, or perceptions of how others view a potential romantic partner (Graziano et al., 1993; Sprecher, 1989). In particular, desirability of a prospective partner may be swayed by peer evaluations of the target's physical attractiveness and other attributes. One limitation of existing research in this area, however, is that the effect of peer influence was examined only with regard to socially normative targets Consequently, it is unclear whether peer influence also extends to perceptions of non-traditional targets (e.g., targets that are of a different race).

We hypothesize that social influence will affect attraction to different-race romantic targets. People likely consider the social acceptability of interracial relationships when evaluating the attractiveness of different race targets, because initiating such relationships may bring certain costs (e.g., discrimination, ostracism). Social comparison information might therefore provide an indicator as to the potential costs incurred if one were to initiate an interracial relationship and indicate when it might be more or less socially difficult to begin such a romance. Thus, when social comparison information is favorable (and perceived costs are low), different-race romantic targets might be seen as more attractive relative to when social comparison information is unfavorable (and perceived costs are high).

Method

White, heterosexual, college undergraduates (N=80; 31 men, 49 women) rated their physical attraction to several prospective targets of the other sex in terms of their degree of physical attractiveness. The photos varied in terms of race (i.e., Black vs. White) and were pretested to be of approximately the same level of physical attractiveness.

Our manipulation consisted of the type of social comparison information (positive, negative, or none) made available to participants before rating each photo. Positive comparison information notified participants that ostensibly similar peers found the target to be relatively attractive; negative comparison information notified participants that such peers found the target to be relatively unattractive. This study involved a within-subjects design. Consequently, every participant rated both Black and White targets and received each form of social comparison information multiple times.

Results

We created attractiveness composite variables for the positive, negative, and no information conditions for the Black and White targets. Thus, we had six dependent variables: Black target/positive information, Black target/negative information, Black target/no information, White target/positive information, White target/negative information, and White target/no information. We then conducted a series of paired t-tests to examine the effectiveness of the various forms of peer comparison information.

When participants received positive social comparison information, they rated the targets as more attractive than when they received negative social comparison information. This was true for both same, t(79) = 7.06, p < .001, and different race targets t(79) = 3.87, p < .001. The magnitude of the effect tended to be stronger for same, as compared to different race targets (see table of means below).

Type of Comparison Information	Race of Target	
	Black	White
Positive	3.57_a	3.95_x
Negative	3.09_b	3.05_y
None	2.88_b	3.28_z

Note: Differing subscripts within columns indicate significant mean differences, p < .05.

Moreover, both positive and negative information had an effect (relative to the no information condition), particularly for same race targets. Finally, none of these effects appeared to be qualified by participant gender.

Discussion

As hypothesized, participants were responsive to social comparison information when making attractiveness ratings, a finding that held true regardless of the race of the target.

However, it is important to note that these data seem to suggest that social comparison information may have somewhat less of an effect for targets of a different race, perhaps because numerous other social psychological factors affect willingness to date interracially (e.g., political ideology, racism, etc.).

In summary, peer influence seems to be an important factor underlying attraction to both traditional and non-traditional romantic relationships. Future research should consider the specific mechanism(s) by which social comparison information affects evaluations of non-traditional targets (e.g., does it influence perceived costs associated with beginning an interracial romance?). In addition, future research might address whether social influence reduces perceived barriers to entering other types of non-traditional involvements (e.g., age-gap, interreligious, etc.).

References

➢ Graziano, W. G., Jensen-Campbell, L., Shebilske, L., & Lundgren, S. (1993). Social influence, sex differences, and judgments of beauty: Putting the 'interpersonal' back in interpersonal attraction. Journal of Personality & Social Psychology, 65, 522-531.

➢ Sprecher, S. (1989). The importance to males and females of physical attractiveness, earning potential and expressiveness in initial attraction. Sex Roles: A Journal of Research, 21, 591-607.

Presented at the 2008 International Association for Relationship Research Conference, Providence, RI

Research Experience Journal

Now that you have almost completed your entire research project, we would like you to reflect on what this experience was like for you. Each of your group members and you will complete this assignment separately. Expect to discuss it at the next class meeting.

1. What aspect of the research process did you enjoy most?

2. What did you find to be the most difficult—or challenging—part of this research?

3. Did you encounter anything unexpected or surprising while carrying out your research?

4. After completing this project, how do you feel about the research process, and psychology as a science? Did anything surprise you about this process?

5. How prepared do you feel to carry out a scientific research project on your own? What more do you feel you need to learn about?

ORAL PRESENTATIONS

Final Presentation Guidelines

For your in-class presentation, your research team and you will present your study to the class using PowerPoint or another presentation program. The format of your presentation should resemble the papers that you are writing. Start with an introduction; describe your procedure and methods; present your results; summarize your findings; and describe the limitations and importance of what you found.

Because this is a semester-long course, and you had limited time to collect data, it is obvious that for *some* lab groups, sample size may be a limitation. However, please keep in mind that sometimes lab groups will state that sample size was an issue, even though it really was not. There are lots of very good published studies in the psychological literature that have had relatively few participants. It is not an ideal situation to have a small number of participants, but it is often a reality in the pursuit of research. Given this likelihood, DO NOT use sample size as a limitation for your presentation. While we would all like to have larger sample sizes in our studies, it should not be the focus and explanation for your results, or lack thereof. Instead, you should focus on the *other* methodological and theoretical limitations of your study.

The second to last page of this lab manual lists the information that should be included in your presentation. Be sure to cover all of the points listed there. You should all present a portion of the talk, and provide handouts for the class. Your presentation should not be longer than 15 minutes.

Helpful pointers:

1. Use large-size font on each slide.
2. Simple slides with less text are usually preferable.
3. Choose colors and font types that are easy to read.
4. Your slides should have a logical and sequential flow.
5. Practice, practice, practice before giving your presentation. so that you do not end up reading each slide word for word on the big day.
6. Make a back-up copy of your presentation; be sure each group member has it.

For additional tips on creating an effective presentation, see: *http://www.columbia.edu/cu/psychology/200bc/present.html*

Lab #29

Purpose:

- Use class time to continue working on your oral presentation with your group.
- Discuss Research Experience Journal.

Objectives:

- Use class time to work on oral presentations.
- Share your experiences about the research process with the class and learn what others' experiences were like.

Homework:

- Prepare to give oral presentation at the next lab.

Lab #30

Purpose:

- Gain experience presenting experimental results to an audience.

Objectives:

- Receive feedback on Discussion section and the abstract.
- Report project results to classmates, in order to share findings of study.
- Practice oral presentation skills.
- Evaluate yourself and your teammates' performance.

Homework:

- The final paper is due at the end of the last lab section meeting time, during finals week.

In-Class Presentation Grading Criteria

Introduction
- Background literature review.
  - Did you discuss how this research builds on prior knowledge?
  - Summarize previous findings and knowledge on this topic. Discuss how this study furthers our understanding of this topic.
- Purpose of study
  - Did you summarize the research question?
  - What ideas were you testing?
  - What theories were guiding your research?
  - What were your hypotheses?

Method and Results
- Summarize the procedure.
  - How did you test your ideas? What was the experimental design? Who were the participants?
  - Did you report a brief summary of the important constructs measured? For instance, "We measured the participants' level of satisfaction, trust, etc.?"
  - Did you NOT spend time discussing the minutiae of each measure taken? For example, "The Hendrick Satisfaction Scale had seven items, which included … ; scores for each item could range 1–7.

Each item was then aggregated to form a single index …" is not appropriate.
- Summarize the findings.
  - What were the IMPORTANT and/or SURPRISING research findings?
  - Did you relate your findings to your hypotheses?
  - Did you NOT give a laundry list of each significant or nonsignificant finding?
    » If you are uncertain which findings to discuss, review the original purpose of the study.

Discussion
- Importance of findings.
  - Why is this study important (i.e., why should we care)?
  - How does this advance our knowledge on this topic?
  - How can we apply this knowledge to the real world?
- Limitations and possible future research directions.
  - What were the drawbacks of your study?
  - Were there design flaws? (Do NOT discuss sample size!)
  - What new questions does your study raise (e.g., future research possibilities)?

Rubric for Assessing Group Members' Ability to Participate Effectively as Part of a Team

Group Topic:_____

Rater:_____ Date:_____

(Circle the appropriate score for each criterion for each member of your group.)

Member Rated (Be sure to rate yourself, too!)	Listening Skills	Openness to others' ideas	Preparation	Contribution	Leadership
	1 2 3 4	1 2 3 4	1 2 3 4	1 2 3 4	1 2 3 4
	1 2 3 4	1 2 3 4	1 2 3 4	1 2 3 4	1 2 3 4
	1 2 3 4	1 2 3 4	1 2 3 4	1 2 3 4	1 2 3 4
	1 2 3 4	1 2 3 4	1 2 3 4	1 2 3 4	1 2 3 4
	1 2 3 4	1 2 3 4	1 2 3 4	1 2 3 4	1 2 3 4
	1 2 3 4	1 2 3 4	1 2 3 4	1 2 3 4	1 2 3 4

Criterion	Excellent (4)	Good (3)	Needs Improvement (2)	Unacceptable (1)
Listening Skills	Routinely restates what others say before responding; rarely interrupts; frequently solicits others' contributions; sustains eye contact	Often restates what others say before responding; usually does not interrupt; often solicits others' contributions; makes eye contact	Rarely restates what others say before responding; often interrupts; rarely solicits others' contributions; does not make eye contact; at times converses with others when another team member is speaking	Does not restate what others say before responding; frequently interrupts; does not solicit contributions from others; is readily distracted; often converses with others when another team member is speaking
Openness to others' ideas	Listens to others' ideas without interrupting; responds positively to the ideas even if rejects; asks questions about the ideas	Listens to others' ideas without interrupting; responds positively to the ideas even if rejects	Interrupts others' articulation of their ideas; does not comment on the ideas	Interrupts others' articulation of their ideas; makes deprecatory comments and/or gestures
Preparation	Always completes assignments; always comes to team sessions with necessary documents and materials; does additional research, reading, writing, designing, implementing	Typically completes assignments; typically comes to team sessions with necessary documents and materials	Sometimes completes assignments; sometimes comes to team sessions with necessary documents and materials	Typically does not complete assignments; typically comes to team sessions without necessary documents and materials
Contribution	Always contributes; quality of contributions is exceptional	Usually contributes; quality of contributions is solid	Sometimes contributes; quality of contribution is inconsistent	Rarely contributes; contributions are often peripheral or irrelevant; frequently misses team sessions
Leadership	Seeks opportunities to lead; in leading is attentive to each member of the team, articulates outcomes for each session and each project, keeps team on schedule, foregrounds collaboration and integration of individual efforts	Is willing to lead; in leading is attentive to each member of the team, articulates general direction for each session and each project, attempts to keep team on schedule	Resists taking on leadership role; in leading allows uneven contributions from team members, is unclear about outcomes or direction, does not make plans for sessions or projects	May volunteer to lead but does not follow through; misses team sessions, does not address outcomes or direction for sessions or projects, team members become anarchical